PENGUIN BOOKS
UNHEARD VOICES

Harsh Mander is a social activist, writer and civil servant. He has worked in Madhya Pradesh and Chhatisgarh for almost two decades. He is closely associated with social causes and movements, for tribal, dalit, disabled, and women's rights, the right to information, custodial justice, bonded labour, land reforms, rights of people displaced by big projects, literacy and health. He writes on social issues. At present he is Country Director of a development support organization, ActionAid India.

Harsh Mander lives with his wife and daughter in New Delhi.

Praise for *Unheard Voices*

'Mander brings out the spirit of resilience and optimism that drive these people who doggedly resist despair . . . (His book) offers a voice to the voiceless. It tells stories which need to be told but, sadly, seldom are.'
—*The Telegraph*

'Mander's collection of 20 tales chronicle the lives of people we know as statistics, not as human beings who retain their dignity and humanism under extremely adverse conditions.'

—*India Today*

'He tells stories that are sad, even tragic, but he doesn't belabour the point. While bringing alive the exceptional circumstances, whether the sectarian violence or famine, that his people recount, what comes through is the story of human courage in the face of impossible odds.'
—Tehelka.com, Literary Review

'What is heartening is that these are all real people and their stories could have been yours.'

—*Indian Express*

'A highly readable collage, with just one grouse. When's the next book coming?'

—*Hindustan Times*

Unheard Voices

Stories of Forgotten Lives

HARSH MANDER

PENGUIN BOOKS

An imprint of Penguin Random House

PENGUIN BOOKS

USA | Canada | UK | Ireland | Australia
New Zealand | India | South Africa | China | Singapore

Penguin Books is part of the Penguin Random House group of companies
whose addresses can be found at global.penguinrandomhouse.com

Published by Penguin Random House India Pvt. Ltd
4th Floor, Capital Tower 1, MG Road,
Gurugram 122 002, Haryana, India

First published by Penguin Books India 2001

Copyright © Harsh Mander 2001

All rights reserved

12 11 10 9 8 7

ISBN 9780141006659

Typeset in Sabon by Mantra Virtual Services, New Delhi

Printed at Repro India Limited

www.penguin.co.in

MIX
Paper from
responsible sources
FSC® C047271

*Dedicated in loving memory to Preet Mander
who was to me sister, mother, mentor and best friend
and who has illuminated all that I have done and
cherished*

Come take,
I have a dream for you.
A dream of jewelled days.
Of winter passing
on to warmth
And drought quenched
by rain.

Come take,
I have a wish for you.
A wish that teaches
all your griefs to laugh.
That heals your wounds
by proudly baring them
to air and warmth.
That takes your pains
for bricks to slowly build
truth's safeguards.

Come take,
I have a gift for you
Of love
And love.
A touchstone.

—Preet Mander (1952-74)

CONTENTS

PREFACE

This is a collection of real-life stories of forgotten women and men, girls and boys, in contemporary India. These are invisible people who in many ways, have been pushed to the extreme edges of society in the name of development and change. Their narratives show not only how they survive and cope; they bring out their endeavour to overcome, with rare and humbling courage, resilience, optimism, humanism and hope.

Among those who populate the pages of this book are street children, sex workers, women, dalit and tribal survivors of atrocities, riot victims, especially women, homeless and destitute people, scavengers of night soil, and those living with leprosy and HIV. There are people displaced by big development projects, and those who have survived recurring famines as in western Orissa, besides monumental disasters like the Bhopal gas leak and the Orissa supercyclone that hit the headlines.

These stories were written at different times, and, initially, not intended as a collection. In all the stories, I have attempted, as authentically as I could, to retain the voices and experiences of the people themselves in the events that unfold. In some of the stories, though, I have altered names and in a few even the locations, to protect identities.

The official designations that appear in some stories

would require explanation for those unfamiliar with rural and small-town India. The SDM, sub-divisional magistrate or sub-collector, is the official charged with administering all development programmes, law and order and land administration in a sub-unit of a district called a sub-division; one sub-division may have even a few hundred thousand people. This is normally the first independent responsibility of a young recruit into the elite Indian Administrative Service. The same responsibilities, but at the heard of a district, which may include some 5,000 villages and towns and a population close to two million people are vested with the collector, also called the DM or district magistrate. The SP or superintendent of police is an equal partner of the DM, and heads the district police force.

ACKNOWLEDGEMENTS

There are a large number of people who made valuable contributions to my research and writing of the stories in this volume. I have acknowledged some of them in the notes on individual stories at the end of the book, but there are many whom it has not been possible to mention by name.

My greatest debt remains to those who agreed to share their stories with me, with candour and faith, despite the pain of several of their memories. This book is a trust to them. If I have been able to do them even the least justice, I would regard my efforts as worth their while.

A special thanks to my many teachers, friends and critics, who encouraged me to write these stories, and gave valuable suggestions. These include Baba Amte, S.R. Sankaran, Shekhar Singh, Aruna Roy, Nikhil Dey, Shankar, N.C. Saxena, Jean Dreze, Pamela Shurmer Smith, Ghanshyam Shah, R. Srinivasa Murthy, Robert Chambers, Usha Ramanathan, Ananthakrishna, Rajni Bakshi, G. Narendranath, Uma Sankari, Mihir Shah, Pradip Prabhu, Shiraz Balsara, Shashi Tharoor, Jharana Jhaveri, Anurag Singh, Vijay Pratap, Vidya Rao, Saeed Mirza, Shyam Benegal, M.J. Akbar, Usha Rai, B.S. Baswan, and many others.

A few of the stories were published in the *Asian Age*, and I am grateful that the newspaper saw value in these stories despite their length and the conventional wisdom that newspaper readers do not have the time for themes related to people living in poverty. Some have also appeared in the *Indian Express* and *Hindustan Times*. An abridged version of the story, 'The Laminated Marksheet' is part of an anthology about the lives of sex workers called *Fallen Angels: The Sex Workers of South Asia*, edited by John Frederick and Thomas Kelly (Roli Books, 2000).

Shyam Benegal, a leading film-maker, based his film *Samar*, on the theme of dalit oppression, on two stories from this collection, 'A Shortlived Revolt' and 'The Obeisance'. It was shot in the village in Sagar district, Madhya Pradesh, in which the events described in the former story actually unfolded. The film went on to win the National Award for the Best Film of 1998, as well as the Award for the Best Screenplay.

In many of the stories, some external social work organizations or committed individuals have played a significant part in assisting the protagonists to overcome their difficult situations. I have taken care to speak about the role of such external actors only to the extent necessary for the story to unfold. The reason is that these stories are not primarily about the support provided by such agencies, either official or non-official. The stories are about the people themselves, who are rarely acknowledged or even visible, and who despite suffering extreme injustice and denial, not only cope but build their lives with rare dignity and affirmation.

A few of the stories are based on events in which I was also involved, as an officer of the Indian Administrative Service, posted in several districts of the sprawling, forested state of Madhya Pradesh. They are 'The Land of Jagtu Gond', 'The Secret Wounds of Jatin', 'The Obeisance', 'The Laminated Marksheet' and 'Together As One People. Although these stories are in a sense autobiographical, they are not intended to be *my* stories, and I hope I have been successful in not allowing myself in any way to overshadow the real protagonists of these stories. I have tried to do this by referring to myself only in the third person, and never by name, only by official designation, and dwelling as little on my personal role except where it is absolutely unavoidable.

Some of the stories in this book while were originally written as case-studies in an effort to make my teaching of young civil servants in the Lal Bahadur Shastri National Academy of Administration, Mussoorie, more effective during my three-year tenure there from 1993-96. I owe a debt to my many students from those days who responded to the stories with commitment and compassion.

Many of the stories were written during my current assignment, as head of a development support organization ActionAid India, on deputation from the Government. A number of my extremely humane and committed colleagues at ActionAid helped me research these stories, and more importantly, to take up programmes to address the injustices that we together have encountered. In my office in ActionAid, I received very special friendship and support for this work from my colleagues Vijay Naugain, Biraj Patnaik and Kavita Kuruganti.

I was fortunate that Raj Kamini Mahadevan and Paul Vinay Kumar of Penguin Books India believed so deeply in what this book stood for. Kamini put in a great deal of effort to improve and polish the final manuscript.

It is usual to acknowledge the support received from one's family in this space. I do so with hesitation for this very reason, but without such a reference this page, indeed would be incomplete. I would only say that the values I cherish and my life's pursuits are inspired by what I learnt from my sister Preet, during her very short life. It is to her memory that this book is dedicated. I have been nourished and supported by the love of my parents, my wife Dimple who has shared both difficult and good times, my brother Raj, and my daughter Suroor, who fills the empty spaces of my heart.

AFTER BHOPAL

The large family was all curled together under quilts when, around midnight, they suddenly woke up with a terrible choking feeling. Neighbours banged on the door shouting, gas has leaked from the factory! Run! Run!

It was the night of 2 December 1984.

Sunil had not wanted to go to bed that night. His bag and uniform were ready for school the following morning. It was Sunday, and he had played all day long with his seven brothers and sisters. Pushpa, his eldest sister, recently married, had returned only a few weeks earlier to her parents' home in Bhopal to celebrate Diwali, and he longed to spend more time with her. Their father was a carpenter, respected for his skills in making furniture, and he earned over a hundred rupees a day. Although it was a large family, Sunil never recalls a day when he went to bed hungry. They lived in a small mud and wood shanty in a slum called JP Nagar. The government had awarded all slum-dwellers tenurial rights for the land on which their homes stood only months earlier.

Outside it was pitch dark, and even the electric lights were shrouded by a dense, deadly fog of poison gas that engulfed the shanty town. JP Nagar was a slum that had been settled haphazardly just adjacent to the Union Carbide Corporation pesticide factory in Bhopal. Unknown to its residents, what had happened that night was that during routine maintenance operations, a large quantity of water had entered one of the storage tanks of the factory, through leaking valves and corroded pipes. The tank contained sixty tonnes of methyl isocyanate (MIC), and the water triggered a runaway chemical reaction, resulting in the discharge of forty tonnes of a lethal combination of MIC, hydrogen cyanide, mono methylamine and carbon monoxide, on a sleeping city of a million unsuspecting people.

One of the first localities into which the gas spewed was JP Nagar, where Sunil and his family were sleeping. Now roused, they found themselves gasping for breath, their eyes burning as if they were on fire. Coughing and screaming, they ran out of their homes, and found themselves swept by a human torrent surging ahead to safety.

Sunil, then eleven years old, tightly held the hand of his younger sister Mamata as he ran desperately. Lost in the dense clouds of gas from the plant, he had got separated from the rest of his family. Suddenly, he badly needed to urinate. He had stopped for barely a moment to do this when even Mamata's hand was wrenched out of his. Screaming people surged from all sides, some fell and were crushed, others tore off their clothes, yet others were vomiting uncontrollably. The stench of urine and shit was overpowering. All around people were collapsing, unconscious or dead.

Sunil ran past the Chhola cremation ground, gasping for his life, his eyes afire, until near a plywood mill he could make out the phantom form of a matador van. The van driver was bundling his family into the van, and Sunil also pushed his way inside. He does not recall how the van-driver manoeuvred his way through the desperate crowds, out of the city, and drove non-stop all the way to the village of Budhni. There was panic in the village that the gas would reach that far, and the van-driver drove on up to the neighbouring town of Hoshangabad. It was close to dawn, on the morning of 3 December 1984, when they reached Hoshangabad. The van-driver left Sunil by a roadside tea stall. Sunil lay down there on the road exhausted, unseeing, and in desperate pain. The local people and policemen picked him up and took him to the district hospital.

There he lay for the next four or five days, his pain slowly becoming more bearable as he was nursed and treated by the hospital staff. But all the while, he was seized by a deep foreboding about what had become of his family. The local administration flashed details about him on the radio. Meanwhile, Sunil's relatives from Lucknow who had heard about the gas tragedy rushed to Bhopal to search for their family members. The radio announcement about Sunil led them to the district hospital in Hoshangabad.

Sunil felt a rush of both relief and panic when he saw his relatives, his mother's brother and sister Pushpa's husband. He asked how the rest of his family was. At that point they hid the terrible truth from him. When he was discharged from the hospital, Sunil's relatives took him back home to JP Nagar. It was like returning to a graveyard. There was loud weeping all around. Relief volunteers were distributing milk and food. Slowly, his relatives broke their silence on the immense tragedy that had befallen them. His mother had died holding her eight-month-old infant son, Sanjay, who miraculously

had survived. The relatives had identified her body in the
Hamidia police station, and had retrieved the baby.
Neighbours reported that their father had returned to
their hut the next morning. On the night of the gas leak,
their father had locked the hut before they ran. When he
opened the door on his return the next morning, he found
the dead body of one of his sons, Santosh, who
accidentally had been left behind in the panic. Shortly
after, their father died, maybe of the gas, maybe of a
broken heart, and the neighbours had cremated him.

Of his seven brothers and sisters, only the baby
Sanjay, and Mamata, whose hand had been wrenched
from his in the crowd, were saved. The bodies of the
others in the family were identified from the posters put
up in the police stations, carrying photographs of the
people who had been cremated on the mass funeral pyres
or buried in mass graves.

Sunil suddenly found himself almost completely alone
in the world. All of eleven years, he was now responsible
for looking after his eight-month-old brother, and his
sister who was three years younger than him. Meanwhile,
rumours swept the stunned and devastated city that while
cleaning out the gas from the factory, there was danger
that gas would leak once again. The chief minister
attempted to counter these rumours with the launch of
what he described as Operation Hope. As part of this
exercise tall screens were erected around the factory and
sprayed by helicopters under the gaze of TV cameras. But
the survivors of Bhopal refused to be reassured or
assuaged, and a second exodus began from the city in the
same month. People sold their belongings, and even their
homesteads, for a pittance, as they fled to safer places.

Sunil's relatives persuaded him to move to Lucknow with his brother and sister. They sold all the belongings of the family in Bhopal, except their home in JP Nagar, and moved there.

But within six months, young Sunil returned to Bhopal. His relatives used his sister Mamata as a servant in their home. Sunil resolved to bring up his younger sister and infant brother, without help from his larger family.

Help did come, mainly from his neighbours in JP Nagar. They fed the children, and took turns to look after the baby. But it was a sombre world to grow up in. In his lane alone, twenty-five people had died. Sounds of weeping were heard from different corners at unexpected hours of the day and night, and a dense mood of grief and despair settled there. Survival in the shanty town was threatened, because those who had inhaled the gas could no longer do physical labour to earn a living, as they had in the past.

In the early years, however, the survivors lived on relief. The efforts of government to rebuild livelihoods of the survivors ended as sad and expensive failures. The Madhya Pradesh government over fifteen years spent 700 million rupees for reconstructing livelihoods, built 152 worksheds, trained about 6,500 people, yet created some kind of on-going livelihoods for little more than eighty women.

Sunil decided not to go back to school, but instead to devote himself entirely to his brother and sister. He recalls with gratitude a young man of JP Colony, Mohammed Ali, who took him under his care, and went with him to various government offices to help him secure his compensation. Initially, for each dead person, the next of kin were given Rs 10,000. There were seven dead in Sunil's family, so he received with Mohammad Ali's help a total of Rs 70,000. Of these Rs 10,000 went to his sister's husband in Lucknow. The rest of the money was placed in fixed bank deposit. Sunil received Rs 580 per month as interest, and on this he brought up his family.

A couple of years passed, and a junior official from the women and child development department of the state government visited Sunil's home, and persuaded him to admit the children in a hostel at Indore. It had been hard for him as a young boy to bring up an infant and a little girl, so Sunil agreed. He went with his brother and sister in a government jeep to Indore, and left them at the hostel. But, Sunil found it painful to return to an empty home.

Meanwhile, unknown to Sunil and other residents of JP Nagar, as they struggled for livelihoods and ways to stem their failing health, a curious legal battle was being fought on their behalf in the courts of India and USA. The Indian government through the Bhopal Gas Leak Disaster (Processing of Claims) Act in March 1985 arrogated to itself, sole powers to represent the victims in the civil litigation against Union Carbide. On behalf of the victims the Indian government filed a suit for compensation of more than 3 billion US dollars in the Federal Court of the Southern District of New York.

In the search for a star witness in New York courts, government officials settled for Sunil, because he was a child who had lost his parents and five brothers and sisters in the tragedy. Government officials, including a senior officer of the district, visited him in his hutment to persuade him to be part of a government team which would travel by aeroplane to New York to give evidence.

Sunil's neighbours clamoured that he should not agree to go to New York. They reasoned with him—once you get on to an aeroplane, who knows whether you would even return home alive.

Sunil was frightened, but also excited, and in the end agreed to fly out to the United States with the Indian team. Government officials accompanied him on the aeroplane to New York. Sunil recalls feeling afraid that his neighbours' warnings would turn out to be true.

At the New York airport, the delegation was received by the Indian ambassador. It was cold. Someone gave Sunil a windcheater. They were put up in a luxurious hotel, and because of jetlag, Sunil spent a lot of his time sleeping during the day, and lay awake, tossing about nervously at night. One evening the ambassador invited the delegation home for a party. Drinks were served, followed by an elaborate dinner.

In court, Sunil told his story fluently in Hindi, and his testimony was translated for the judge. He learnt later that the case was returned in May 1986 to the Indian courts on grounds of 'forum non-convenience', under the condition that Union Carbide would submit to their jurisdiction. During the proceedings at the Bhopal district court, Union Carbide was directed to pay an interim relief sum of Rs 3,500 million so that the delay in the adjudication of the case did not adversely affect the claimants.

However, Union Carbide refused to pay interim relief and its appeal against this decision reached the Indian Supreme Court. On 14 February 1989, in a sudden departure from the matter of interim relief, the Supreme Court passed an order approving the settlement that had been reached between the Government of India and Union Carbide, without the knowledge of the claimants of Bhopal. According to the terms of the settlement, in exchange of payment of 470 million US dollars, the Corporation was to be absolved of all liabilities, criminal cases against the company and its officials were to be dropped, and the Indian government was to defend the Corporation in the event of future suits. The settlement sum, nearly one-seventh of the damages initially claimed by the government, while being far below international standards was, in fact, even lower than the modest standards set by the Indian Railways for railway accidents. There were widespread protests by the Bhopal victims against the betrayal by the government and many organizations and individuals including prominent members of the parliament supported the call to oppose the infamous settlement. Several petitions seeking review of the order on settlement were filed and the Supreme Court announced its revised judgement on 3 October 1991. The final judgement upheld the settlement amount paid by Carbide but directed the Indian government to make good any shortfall during the distribution of compensation. Also the criminal cases against the Corporation and its officials were reinstated in the final judgement. The Supreme Court also directed Union Carbide to finance a 500-bed hospital for the medical care of the victims.

After receiving so much attention from the Indian government authorities during the court case, Sunil found himself forgotten after he returned to India. The SOS Villages of India established a settlement in Bhopal, and his brother and sister were transferred there. Sunil was permitted to meet them once a month, and he greatly looked forward to these visits. These were moments of light amidst his loneliness.

It was once again Sunil's older friend, Mohammad Ali, who assisted him to secure his full claims from the maze of the Bhopal settlement courts. Mohammad Ali, who worked in a cloth mill, would take time off from work to accompany Sunil whenever he had a date with the courts.

But, over time, it became increasingly difficult for Sunil to return to his empty house. It was too full of memories. His brother and sister were growing up in the SOS Village. Activists working with gas relief had constituted a group called Children Against Carbide. Sunil recalls his time with this group, both for the excitement he experienced while organizing protest rallies, as well as for the companionship it offered him. In time, in 1991, he moved in to stay with a leading activist Sathyu. A year later, in 1992, the state government built a 'widows' colony'. Houses were allotted by lottery to widows and orphans who had survived the Bhopal gas tragedy, and Sunil qualified. He then moved into this colony, where he lives until today.

Sunil finally was awarded a compensation of seven hundred thousand rupees. One hundred thousand he invested in purchasing a mini-bus, the remaining he put in a bank to secure the future of his brother and sister. The mini-bus brought him four to five thousand rupees a month for six months. Then one day, the driver and conductor were caught smuggling opium in the bus, and it was seized by the police.

By now, Sunil had reached manhood. Many people sought to befriend him, because after receiving his compensation, he had became a man of uncommon means. He began drinking, and the habit increasingly took hold of him. Perhaps, it filled a certain emptiness than lay within him.

One day, some friends persuaded him to join a Hindu communal organization in Bhopal. You have a good strong body, they told him. Why don't you do something for your community. He spent a year with the organization, and it brought him the company of many young men. But Sunil recalls that there was so much hatred, so many untruths against the Muslim community, that in the end he decided to part ways with the organization.

In 1994, his sister turned eighteen, beyond the protection offered by the SOS Village in Bhopal. Sunil decided to get both his sister and brother discharged from the SOS Village, and they moved in with him, in the widows' colony.

Their presence filled a little bit the accumulated loneliness that festered inside his soul all these years. But perhaps they returned too late. Member of the Hindu communal organization of which he had been a member continued to meet him, encouraging him to drink, and pressurizing him to spend the large sums of compensation money which lay in the bank in his name. But he was adamant that he would not withdraw this money, which he saw as a trust for the future of his brother and sister. His relationship with the member of the organization soured and they spread ugly and shameful rumours about Sunil's character.

As time passed, Sunil became more and more withdrawn and uncommunicative. Slowly, almost imperceptibly, he found something slowly cracking up within him. He was frequently depressed, and became obsessed by thoughts of suicide. He heard voices call out to him. He would not stir out of his home, would not wash himself or talk to people. The neighbours took care of his brother and sister, and fed Sunil. As his condition worsened, they contacted his activist friend of the past, Sathyu, who once again took him into his home and had him treated. There were times when he ran out of the house without clothes, feverishly roaming the streets night and day, running for kilometres on the railway track into the forest.

For the four years prior to the writing of this piece, Sunil has been on medication for his mental illness. He moved back to his home in the widows' colony with his brother and sister. He lives and supports his family on the interest earned by the compensation money in the bank. He continues to refuse to touch the principal; he is uncompromising that this is for when they grow up. He refuses also to consider marriage for himself. He must first ensure a good future for those he had taken fifteen years earlier under his care.

Two years ago, he got his sister Mamata married. His relatives in Lucknow found a suitable boy for her there, an electrician by trade. His brother studies in an English-medium school, Sunil says with pride, and he gets good marks. I want to be an engineer, the brother says shyly. He has come a long way from the infant in his mother's arms, on the winter night of 1984 that changed their lives forever.

Sunil's eyes look glazed, without expression, empty of

emotion and warmth, as he speaks sparingly. But during our meeting, there was one time when they lit up, and he smiled. This was when he spoke to us of his sister Mamata's visit home last year for Holi. She had brought home her first-born child. What a beautiful child he is, Sunil said. So fair, and with eyes shaped like a *kairee,* a young mango, he added with pride and tenderness.

And in this way, life does go on.

HOUNDED LIKE CRIMINALS

The only organized red light area in the city of Hyderabad was Mehboob-ki-Mahendi, located near the historic Char Minar. This was a densely populated part of the old city. Out of rented premises there, interspersed between residential and business establishments, around a hundred women plied their trade at any point of time, supervised closely by brothel-keepers or *sethanis*, and supported by a shadowy network of financiers, pimps and policemen.

Among the women who once worked there was Nirmala. She was born in Madurai. Her mother died while bringing her into the world, and her father left her and her sister with his married sister, never turning back to ensure, or to even enquire about her welfare. Her aunt brought them up with love and care, despite herself being in penury. Nirmala studied up to high school, when she developed a relationship with a neighbourhood garage mechanic. He married her against his parents' wishes, but later abandoned her. She was seven months pregnant at the time. Soon after she gave birth to a healthy baby boy. When her son was only four months old, she went with him to Kerala, then to Hyderabad in search of work. In Hyderabad, her mother's sister gave her shelter and found her employment as a domestic servant.

The boy grew up, clinging to the saree edge of his mother as she toiled in people's homes, until he was old enough to go to school. Nirmala wanted the best education for him. She took him to Ootacamund, where her sister had married. Her brother-in-law helped her secure admission for her son in a Christian missionary boarding school. She promised her brother-in-law that she would regularly send him money for the fees. She assured her family that she had a well-paying job. The only problem was that as she was rarely given leave, the boy would have to stay on in the hostel even during the school holidays. But she did promise to visit him at least twice a year.

Leaving him in the hostel, she went straight to Bombay. Over the past few years she had thought hard and deep about her circumstances, and had made up her mind about how she wanted to earn the money needed to educate her son and support herself. A friend had given her the address of a brothel in the infamous red-light area of the city. She proceeded to the place, and there she remained for nearly seven years. This was in 1990.

When we met her later in Hyderabad, to where she had moved, she was reluctant to talk very much about her years of work in Bombay. We did not want to press her. All that emerged from her account was that she had no regrets about the choices she had made. She endearingly referred to her periods of sex work as her phases of 'fieldwork'. In my own work both in government or with voluntary organizations, the term 'fieldwork' has the soft halo of service to people in need. Perhaps for high-school educated Nirmala, it had connotations that were not dissimilar!

A friend advised her that prospects were better in Mehboob-ki-Mahendi, the red-light area in the burgeoning twin cities of Hyderabad and Secunderabad. In the spring of 1997, she set herself up in that brothel near the Char Minar. The terms were the same. Half her earnings went to the *sethani* who managed the brothel; the rest she could retain. She now made new friends among the women there, and settled down to start another phase of her 'fieldwork'.

Within barely a fortnight of her stay in the new establishment, there was chaos one night. It was 19 April 1997. On the orders of the court, the premises were raided to 'rescue' the brothel's inmates. Nirmala and other women remembered that night as a terrifying, blind orgy of violence, in which residents of neighbouring houses joined the police in raiding and smashing all their belongings, including their television set, and furniture. Their personal effects and cash were looted. The premises were gutted. The inmates put up a spirited fight. Nirmala recalls with satisfaction grabbing a policeman by his collar, and tearing his shirt right down to his trousers, and the uncontrolled fury he unleashed on her in response. The place was later gutted as 12 May 1997, in another 'clean-up operation' led by the local assistant commissioner of police.

Unknown to Nirmala, just a month earlier, a resident of the city named Swamy, a member of what he described as the 'Labour Liberation Front', wrote a letter to the High Court demanding an end to the 'social evil of prostitution'. He pleaded for the forceful removal of the red-light area from Mehboob-ki-Mahendi, and the 'rescue' of the women engaged in sex work. It is difficult to confirm Swamy's motives in making this application, although there was some speculation that the windfall profits from the sale of premises that would be vacated by the brothels could have played a role. Whatever his motives, the High Court admitted this letter as a writ petition, and called for a detailed report from the police.

Meanwhile, around one hundred and eighty individual residents of the Mahendi area impleaded themselves as parties to the case. In their petition to the court, they described the misery of the residents of the area, stating that 'in view of their residences near the area, even the matrimonial alliances to the young girls (sic) have become difficult and they were being doomed and cursed for no fault of theirs. The entire locality had earned the dubious distinction for itself though prostitution was carried on in a few houses in the area.' It urged that the government take steps to stamp out the flesh trade in Mehboob-ki-Mahendi area to 'retrieve the dignity of women.'

A women police officer, Tej Deep, superintendent of police, Women Protection Cell, CID, Hyderabad, visited the premises on 13 April 1997 in compliance with the court's orders. According to her report, one hundred and fifty sex workers were organized into small groups under twenty sethanis, and these brothel-keepers retained half the incomes of the sex workers, in return for which they provided the women with clients and protection. Tej Deep also reported to the court that two financiers advanced sums of money at exorbitant rates of interest to the sex workers, and recovered these from their earnings. The sex workers also contributed to the highly inflated rents paid daily to the twenty-three owners of the premises. Her report also identified two head constables, two constables and two home guards who had 'established a liason' with sex workers of the area and were providing them protection and advance information about police raids.

The violence of these raids, the official and judicial sanction, and glare of·media publicity, all combined to ensure that a lethal blow was dealt to sex work in Mehboob-ki-Mahendi. However, as reported in an investigative report by researcher Kuppili Padma in 1999, sex work continued after the 1997 raid, but in clandestine independent establishments and, to a great extent, on the streets. After the high-profile closure of Mehboob-ki-Mahendi, most women now seek clients away from their living places, so as to avoid the objections from their neighbours. Many women ply their trade in open public places, government offices that fall vacant at night, railway compartments, or places near railway stations.

To return to Nirmala's story, she and the sixty-four other 'rescued' sex workers found conditions in the welfare home in which they were housed unbearable. They felt lonely, and acutely worried about their future. Nirmala was desperate because she could not send back the monthly fees for her son's education. She wrote to her brother-in-law that she was having difficulties at work ; he reassuringly wrote back that he would take care of the fees and she could pay him back in better times.

The physical conditions in the home were subhuman, the food inadequate and poorly cooked, and the staff there treated the women with indignity. The women were unwilling to accept this without a fight. Twelve women ran away, the others decided to go on a spirited—and noisy—protest hunger-strike. To add to the melodrama, they threatened to electrocute themselves if things did not get better. The media got wind of the juicy story, and government was increasingly embarrassed.

The state authorities confabulated on how they could cope with this extraordinary situation. Ensuring that conditions in the state government welfare home for women should be expeditiously improved does not seem to have even been considered as a feasible option, for some unstated reason. Instead, an innovative proposal was made, to shift the women from the welfare home to the women's ward of a jail. It is ironical that conditions in the jail, which are universally acknowledged to be abysmal, were deemed better than those in a welfare home, which was established for the rehabilitation of women in special difficulties. However, this irony seemed to have escaped both the state authorities and the court. The High Court willingly approved the proposal to shift the group of sex workers to the Chenchalguda jail.

Once again, the women encountered insects in their rice, the foul stench of uncleaned bathrooms, and harsh custodial wardens. But they had learned a good lesson from their earlier experience of the welfare home. And so they vociferously protested, threatening once again to go on a hunger-strike if things did not get better. The jail authorities decided to take no chances with this colourful and volatile group of women, who could begin swearing and cursing loudly at the slightest provocation. Steps were taken to ensure that conditions improved quickly, if not greatly, but just enough to become bearable.

The police authorities were then confronted by another challenge. The ways of the courts were whimsical, and there was a possibility that the High Court could at any time order the release of the women. In order to ensure that the women were retained in jail, the police authorities decided that they should also be charged with some criminal offence. After some deliberation the crime selected to book them under was attempted suicide, the grounds being their notorious hunger-strike in the welfare home. Every fifteen days, the women were produced before a magistrate in the district courts. Each time, they would raise a din, shout abuses and throw chappals at him, vociferously demanding that they be released because they had committed no crime. In subsequent hearings the hapless magistrate ordered that the women must leave their chappals outside the courts, so that they would not be able to fling them around. Undeterred, the women cried out in one voice that since even the sethanis had been given bail, there was no reason that they should remain incarcerated.

Meanwhile, there was another development which rendered the chances of their release even bleaker. On the basis of another plea from the state authorities, and explicit orders from the High Court, the women in the jail were forcibly tested for HIV and other sexually-transmitted diseases. Twenty-one women, including Nirmala, were diagnosed to be HIV positive, and seventeen others were found to be infected with other sexually transmitted diseases. The court directed that the sex workers not suffering from any disease be released after executing bonds, but those suffering both from HIV and sexually-transmitted diseases should continue to be detained. Two of the four minor girls were found to be pregnant by three months. Four months later, the court ordered that they should be counselled and their pregnancy be terminated. Fortunately, the court's orders were not obeyed, and the girls delivered their babies later that year.

For the women who were left in jail, life seemed to have reached a dead end. A young woman Radha, with a tumour in her stomach, stopped eating and began visibly wasting away. She was eventually offered bail, but refused, insisting that she would leave only if all her sisters were also released. One night, her situation deteriorated sharply, and she was shifted to hospital. The next morning, the women learnt that she had died. They were grief-stricken, and despair pushed itself deeper into their hearts. They once again went on a hunger-strike, this time to demand that Radha's body be handed over to the young man she loved, Akbar, an auto-rickshaw driver. The jail authorities relented, and the women had the satisfaction that the last rites of Radha were at least not performed by the cold hands of strangers.

In the High Court, the amicus curiae, literally 'friend of the court' appointed to assist to the court, appealed that the rescued women must be released immediately as they had not committed any crime, and that they were being confined wrongfully. Further, he added, that it was not confirmed that they suffered from AIDS, apart from the women who had been forcefully tested HIV positive. Even if the women had tested HIV positive, they could not be incarcerated or isolated, because this would deprive them of the constitutional rights of liberty and free movement. He also pleaded that confining the women any longer would prevent them from looking after their children, who would, consequently, languish.

However, the government pleader vociferously opposed all this. As summarized in a judgement of the

High Court, his argument was that 'if the women are released there is every possibility of going to the same profession as Sethanis and brokers will drag them into the same profession. The rescued women will become the victims by losing their right and dignity of womenhood. The women who are infected with HIV would continue the prostitution, and the HIV will be infected to other persons who participate in the intercourse with them and the same will cause a greater harm to the society.' (sic).

The High Court seemed more influenced by the impassioned arguments of the government pleader than of the amicus curiae. In an extensive judgement delivered on 9 December 1997, the learned judge of the High Court expressed repeated concern for the conditions of the 'poor, weak and fallen women'. He emphasized the role of the state to 'take steps to wipe out the immoral activity of the Society' (sic) and to rehabilitate the victims. He contended that Section 17 (4) of the Immoral Traffic (Prevention) Act, 1956 empowers the magistrate to send the rescued women to the protective homes or welfare homes for their rehabilitation, and for social good, and is, therefore, not violative of their fundamental rights.

However, whereas this section does not make any distinction between women with or without HIV, the learned judge directed that the women without HIV be released on personal bond because they wanted to go home and live with their children and lead a normal life. But for the twenty-one women who had been diagnosed as HIV positive, his order was that they be sent to welfare homes. In the light of the report of the amicus curiae, that minimum facilities were still not available in the state government welfare homes, the court directed the government to consider entrusting this task instead to reputed voluntary organizations.

There were many NGOs that were only too keen to take on this responsibility. Some of them had already directly contacted the women in jail, and were pressing the jail authorities for the women they wanted. The NGOs quarrelled and bargained among themselves. Nirmala said, it felt as if they were *chana* (horse-gram) to be distributed. The NGO selected finally by the state authorities was Pratyamnaya. The state government sanctioned an initial grant of fifteen lakh rupees, apart from giving them possession of a large government building, on an eight-acre site, on the outskirts of the city. The eagerness of the NGOs to take over the women in this high-profile case was not without reason.

Mysterious—and chaotic—are sometimes the ways of governments and courts. At the same time that the High Court passed orders for the continued detention of the HIV positive sex workers in a welfare home, the local court which was trying them for attempt to suicide, resolved finally to release them on a personal bond.

Eight months of incarceration—and young Radha's death—had taken its toll of their spirit. Nirmala recalls with shame and indignation that before their release from jail, all the women diagnosed with HIV were photographed like criminals, holding boards with their names written in bold letters. This is the practice employed conventionally by the police to keep a public record of repeat offenders. The jail authorities also meticulously noted down details of their families, and the addresses they could be located at.

Almost immediately after their release, the state authorities received the High Court order that the women with HIV should continue to be detained in a welfare home. They were deeply embarrassed, when they had to report back to the High Court that all the women had been released, and they feared the uproar that could be created if the media learned of this. The local police was therefore directed to locate the women, wherever they had gone, and to bring them back at any cost.

What followed was a sustained operation by the police to hunt out each of the women, and to ensure their return to custody. In the neighbourhoods where they had begun living, the police stormed in, displaying blown-up pictures of the women holding their name boards, like criminals. The pictures were shown to the neighbours, and the policemen informed them that the women were suffering from a dangerous illness, and that the entire colony would be at risk. The neighbours then angrily demanded of the women that they should pack up and leave at once. If the women still resisted, the men they were living with were beaten up.

Nirmala had moved in with an old male friend who worked as a cook in a hostel. He was an alcoholic who gave up drinking after meeting Nirmala, and loved her dearly. He was badly thrashed by the police because she refused to go with them. She jeered at the three policemen who had hunted her down, particularly because she recognized one of them as her old client. Somehow he knew about her son studying in the boarding school in Ootacamund, and threatened to expose her profession and infection to her son and the school authorities.

Nirmala knew she was defeated; she had no choice but to return with the policeman.

The woman-hunt launched by the police was successful. Within one month, eight women with HIV were back in their net, and placed in the custody of the NGO Pratyamnaya.

The food was better in the centre run by the NGO, than in the state welfare home and jail, and there were even sporadic and desultory attempts to engage them in painting and singing, literacy classes and the making of fruit jam. The trainers were all men, and they were constantly curious about the past lives of these women, who their clients were, what sexual demands they made on them, whether they were violent with them and so on. The women knew that one and a half million rupees had been granted to the NGO by the government for the care of eight of them. It worked out to over one lakh fifty thousand rupees per woman. Occasionally, the women asked the NGO workers awkward questions about where the money had gone. They never received a satisfactory answer.

Nirmala and the other women increasingly became depressed and lonely. They longed for freedom, and intensely missed their families. Nirmala was again unable to send money for her son's education, but her supportive brother-in-law, to whom she wrote that hard times were persisting and she remained out of work, continued to pay his fees. But she longed to see her son's face, and to hold him to her breast.

Geeta, one of the women held in custody in the NGO home, received news that her mother had died because there was no one to care for her. She was half-crazed with worry about her ailing father, who was now all alone. She smashed her glass bangles and threatened to eat the pieces if she was not released. They sent her back to the village, but her father died soon after.

Twenty months of custody passed slowly. Throughout this period, some sensitive activists, lawyers and journalists took up the women's case in the media, and in court, pleading that the liberty of innocent women could not be withheld indefinitely. It took a long time, but the high profile of the case, and the arguments placed before it, persuaded the High Court to finally relent, and the women at last were released.

Once free, the women picked up the threads of their lives in different ways. One of them, Mumtaz married an auto-rickshaw driver and it is rumoured that she has become a sethani. Some are living alone and working in new professions, others have returned to their families, or are living with male friends.

Nirmala decided not to return to her 'fieldwork'. The NGO Pratyamnaya has assisted her with a loan of twenty thousand rupees, and she has set up a small tea-stall. The government has not given her any land on lease to run the tea-stall, but she has encroached on a small plot by the roadside, and plies her new trade there. The NGO also runs a nursery, and she goes there to supplement her income.

While she was in the NGO rehabilitation centre, some members of the Sisters of Charity had left a baby girl infected with HIV at the home. The child's middle-class parents, both of whom were infected with HIV, had abandoned her just after her birth at the hospital itself. The hospital authorities had handed her over to the Sisters of Charity, but the sisters were unwilling to bring up the child. They said they did not have either the facilities or the training to look after a child living with HIV, and they could not allow her to live with other children in their orphans' home. They decided instead to leave the baby in the care of the NGO.

Nirmala volunteered spontaneously to look after the child, whom they called Lucy, in the home itself. She took the little girl with her when she was released from the home. Lucy is now two years old, a laughing child with black luminous eyes. She spends the entire day playing in the mud near Nirmala's tea-stall, under her watchful gaze.

A HOME ON THE STREETS

Anand was only eight years old when he left his home for the streets of Bangalore. Today, twelve years later, he looks at you straight in the face, with clear sparkling eyes, and exudes a quiet, shy confidence. He has his own dreams for the future, and he is determined to achieve them.

Like so many other street children, Anand left home, a small village in Chittoor district of Andhra Pradesh, to escape neglect and abuse in the family. His father was a humble, travelling, village goldsmith. He had no land but his trade ensured that he could make both ends meet. Being constantly on the move because of his father's business, Anand did not have a steady schooling. Yet, he somehow managed to pass his second class examination.

Ever since Anand could remember, his parents would have violent fights. Frequently, his father would brutally beat up his mother. Finally, one day, he threw her out. The two children were left behind, Anand was then six years old and his sister, older by two years. Where his mother went, Anand does not know. She did not return and Anand never saw her again.

Before long, his father brought home another woman. Anand only remembers that she hated the children, gave them stale food, and beat and abused them. He complained to his father, and although he tried to intervene, nothing changed when he was away. Anand then made up his mind to run away. His chance came one day when his father's business brought him to Bangalore. That morning, he quietly walked away from his family, determined that he would never return.

The whole day the eight-year-old boy walked the streets of the metropolis. By evening, he was tired, lonely and hungry. A vegetable and fruit vendor passed by, pushing his hand cart as he headed homewards after the day's work. Anand asked him for some rotting vegetables that had been pushed into a corner of the cart, to be fed to cattle.

The vegetable vendor asked him who he was, and why he was alone in the streets. Anand lied that both his parents were dead, and that he had no home and family. The man took pity on the boy, and took him home to his wife.

Anand recalls that they had no children of their own and were kind to him, and he in turn helped them in hawking vegetables for the next six months. But, in time, he found out that the woman engaged in what Anand called 'side-business'. I did not understand what Anand meant, until I saw that he was embarrassed and shuffled his feet when I pressed him for more details. It was clear that the young boy had lost his innocence quite early. The man was an alcoholic and every other night he would come home reeking of country liquor, and would shout and swear, abuse and beat his wife. One day after a particularly sordid scene, which attracted a crowd of neighbours, the drunken man cursed his wife in the filthiest language, and then completely stripped. Anand decided that he must leave again. He had not abandoned the hell of one home only to enter that of another.

So he was on the streets once again. It was night, and as he wandered aimlessly he came upon some boys with ragged clothes and grimy faces at a street corner. Some were stretched out and sleeping on the pavement, others, in small groups, were eating, playing cards, or simply chatting and laughing.

Anand squatted some distance away, watching them. After a while loneliness and hunger overpowered him and he began to weep quietly. An older boy came up to him. He gave him food and asked him his story. Anand readily unburdened himself. The boy told him they worked as ragpickers, and invited Anand to join them. Next morning, he bought a gunny bag for Anand and taught him the basics of their trade.

The ragpickers spent their day searching in rubbish heaps, salvaging whatever they could of value. Pockets were sewn on the inside of their gunny bags, to store different categories of waste. When the gunny bags were full, the boys would sell what they had collected to the *kabaddi* waste recycling shops—60 paise per kilogram for paper, 3 rupees for iron and 4 rupees for plastic bags. At the end of the day, the ragpickers would earn anything between ten to a hundred rupees from their day's scouring of the rubbish heaps around the city.

The group of ragpickers easily accepted Anand, and his loneliness vanished. Each of the boys bore a tale of tragedy, of which they spoke only occasionally. For many the choice of a life on the streets was a response to brutal physical, sometimes sexual abuse in the family; the bodies of some of the boys bore permanent scars of their brutalization. With some it was emotional neglect; one boy had run away from an elite boarding school in a South Indian hill station, because he felt that his parents did not really love him. With others, it was sheer destitution at home, drunken fathers, large families, unemployment, extreme poverty; the boys left home because of the constant nagging hunger in their stomachs. It was only a few who came for the adventure, the excitement, the lure of city lights.

But, despite being forced to make the streets their home, there was little place in these boys' lives for melancholy, for self-pity. Their existence had an almost compulsive cheerfulness, the desire to live for the here and now. Whatever they earned, they spent. If there was money left over after food which they bought from roadside vendors, they would splurge, on films—sometimes seeing three a day—on clothes, on restaurants, on gambling and on drugs.

Soon enough, Anand was initiated into drugs. He learned to smoke ganja, besides drinking country liquor, and sniffing petrol. Fortunately, he stayed away from harder drugs; perhaps there was some instinct working inside, to save himself for a better life. But the drugs that he took gave him a feeling of lightness, of freedom, and also of camaraderie, as he lay with his friends on the pavement at night, covered with ragpicking gunny bags, searching for stars in the sky dulled and obscured by the harsh lights of the city.

The boys were frequently harassed by older men of the streets, petty criminals, whom Anand described as 'rowdies'. They snatched away their money, and sexually molested them. The boys learned to be nimble on their feet, running into narrow alleys and hiding in the shadows, whenever they saw their older tormentors.

The same nimbleness came handy whenever they encountered their other main oppressors, the police. According to Anand and other street boys, the men in khaki regularly sought out groups of children on the streets as soft targets. If they caught them, they thrashed them, and threatened to throw them in the police lock-up or in the dreaded remand homes for juvenile delinquents. They would free them only if they parted with all their money, and promised to give more in the future. But the boys of the street quickly learnt the skill of staying out of the reach of the unsteady arm of the law, mainly by the speed of their escape at the first sign of khaki.

In the course of ragpicking, Anand encountered Swami who was to become his closest friend. He was already in his late twenties, much older than the other boys in the group, but he was mentally challenged. Anand was attracted by his gentleness, his open, affable nature, and his goodwill to all. They soon became inseparable, and were together at work, eating, watching films, sleeping side by side under the open sky. On the streets, most relationships are transient, but Anand's friendship with Swami has survived all these years. This is despite Swami remaining a ragpicker to this day, while Anand has struggled and secured a better life.

After he had worked as a ragpicker for almost a year, a pavement vegetable vendor who had watched Anand and found him to be a responsible young fellow, offered him employment. He would have to guard the stocks of unsold vegetables at night, sleeping on top of them, and in the mornings help the vegetable vendor with hawking his wares. For this he would get twenty rupees a day, with lunch. This was much less than what he usually earned as a ragpicker. Besides, he would have to leave his new found friends, including Swami whose sluggishness and absence of ambition made him stick to ragpicking. But little Anand wanted a better life and it seemed to him that the vegetable vendor's offer was a new opportunity.

Anand worked with him for about six months, and then in a cycle repair shop. But the cycle repair shop closed down, and Anand was back on the streets. He joined his old friends and returned to ragpicking.

It was then that he first heard of Father George and the shelter for street children that he had started. The Father asks nothing of you, he was told. You can go there whenever you like, to sleep under a roof, to bathe and use the toilet, or to play carrom. Anand decided to give it a try—and after four years as a street child, he first encountered BOSCO, the Bangalore Oniyavara Seva Coota. And it is this that helped him change the direction of his life.

It was in 1980, even before he was ordained as a priest, that George Kollashany and his colleagues began working among ragpickers, coolie-boys, street hawkers, shoe-shine boys, hotel boys, street beggars, and so on. Through repeated contacts they built up relationships of friendship and trust, and shared the daily lives and struggles of these children of the streets. The boys would derive pleasure from taking Father to a tea-shop, as they told him of their past, their struggles and their hopes, and then insist on paying the bills. The volunteers provided on the streets itself, medical and de-addiction facilities, counselling services, intervention with the law-enforcement machinery and the children's employers. They would also try to re-establish contact with the estranged families of the children; eventually some were re-united with them.

These efforts, to reach the children on the streets itself, resulted in George breaking some of the conventions of his religious order. But, they were pioneering in their non-institutional approach to the care and rehabilitation of street children.

The basic philosophy of Father's work is that as long as society remains as it is we will continue to have street children. It is then important to concentrate on reaching them a range of supportive and rehabilitative services. Father also clearly perceived that it would be futile, or at best symbolic, to concentrate one's efforts on a small number of children who are artificially transplanted from their street reality into a protected environment. Any work with street children must respect, and build upon the love of these children for freedom, and their fierce independence.

His approach, instead, is to meet the children as they step out of their homes on to the streets, and to partner them in their daily struggles to survive and grow on the streets. It is based on the belief that a child who refuses to succumb passively to trauma and oppression in the home, has special qualities of courage, and love of liberty and life. As one Father put it, 'As I shared the life of the children on the street, I have been very much enriched by them. Their sense of freedom, their sense of joy, their very lifestyle . . . have all made a deep impression on me. They are boys who courageously moved out of their unbearable home environment for a better life. And on the street they make adult decisions regarding their work, shelter, clothes, food, etc. These "little men" deserve our respect, love and concern.'

Volunteers of the organization, therefore, seek to reach out to these children on the street in a non-judgemental, supportive way, eliciting their friendship and trust, and gradually providing them with hope of support in their efforts to build a better life for themselves. Nothing is imposed on the street children, nor is their freedom forcibly thwarted. Only the possibility of alternatives is presented, and assistance to reach any of them provided, as and when the children so choose.

At the same time, without adult protection, street children, despite their superficial semi-adult street wisdom, are constantly vulnerable, to exploitation and harassment, to hunger, to illness, to drugs, and to loneliness and so on. They lack reliable and humane adult role models. And it is this adult support that the volunteers try to provide the children in their daily life struggles.

The initiative for setting up a shelter was part of such support, in order to enable the children to have the choice to move away from the streets. The shelters are open and unrestricted and the boys can come and go, as and when they please. In a shelter that I visited, some children were stretched out and sleeping, others were bathing, still others were playing carrom, or just laughing and chatting, and a bunch was dancing to the parody of a popular Hindi film song. It was into such a shelter that Anand stumbled four years after he had made the streets of Bangalore his home.

After he had spent the nights for a week there, Father George spoke to Anand. He asked him about his past, his experiences on the streets, and gradually about what he wanted to do. Anand said that most of all he wanted to study. Father arranged for his enrollment as a private student in the seventh standard, but because he had not studied for so long and was still not fluent in Kannada, he failed in three subjects. Father, however, ensured that he did not feel discouraged, and arranged for his admission in a middle-class convent school.

Anand adjusted fast to life in the strange school environment. A boy from a middle-class family mocked him once and tore his book; Anand recalls with satisfaction that while that boy failed his examination, he had passed his. But in his school, by and large, Anand did not experience any discrimination. He became close friends with two boys and even used to visit their homes.

A year later, however, he was once again seized by a restlessness and a longing for freedom. One day he ran away to Mysore. He had confided where he was going to his friend, and to his surprise, four days later, he found Father looking for him near the bus stand at Mysore, where he was sleeping. He was gentle with Anand, and persuaded him to return to school. After that Anand studied without break until he passed high school.

During the holidays that year, the volunteers of the organization said that they had been able to locate his family, and asked whether he would like to go to see his father. Anand agreed, and went with Father to the village shop in which his father was working. His father did not recognize the strapping young lad who stood before him, but was overjoyed to see the son whom he had lost all hope of meeting again. Anand stayed with his family for six months, then returned to Bangalore to find a job. He now maintains regular contact with his family, and returns to be with his father whenever he can find the time.

Anand worked for a while on a construction site. But Father George helped him to get a job as an office boy in a private company. Anand recently decided to go with Father to Hospet, where the organization has opened a vocational centre for training street youth for self-employment.

For all the years he was a child of the streets, Anand had two ambitions. He wanted to be either a policeman, or if that was not possible, a criminal. These two choices may appear paradoxical at one level but are not really so, because the two vocations represent the ultimate symbols of power to a street boy.

Today his ambitions are different. He wants to start an electrical repair shop of his own. His fondest dream is to be able to provide employment to a few more boys who, like him, are forced to make the streets their home.

SCAVENGER NARAYANAMMA

Narayanamma's day begins the same way every morning. She wakes up long before dawn, dresses hurriedly, and rushes off, so that she is on time for the roll-call taken by the municipal inspector, outside the municipal school, before 5 a.m. She then proceeds to her allotted place of duty, searching on the way for large leaves or waste paper to line her basket. The only other tools she needs for her job—a flat, tin plate and broom—she holds under her arm.

There is always a large crowd of women waiting for their turn, a small pot or tin of water, held by the rim, in one hand, outside the municipal toilet where Narayanamma works. It has more than 400 seats, arranged in rows, for the women to squat. Open to the sky and to each other, the toilets are protected from curious eyes by a high wall. It is an old facility, maybe a hundred years old, but it still functions.

From time to time, after the women using the toilet file out, Narayanamma and her fellow workers are called inside. There is no flush. The shit only piles up at each seat, or flows into open drains. It is Narayanamma's job to collect it with her broom on to the flat, tin plate, and pile it into her basket. When the basket is filled, she carries it on her head to a waiting tractor trolley parked at a distance of half a kilometre. And then she is back, waiting for the next call from the toilet. This goes on until about ten in the morning, when at last Narayanamma washes up, and returns home.

Narayanamma is among the estimated one million workers, who continue be employed in what is considered the lowest of all hereditary occupations in the Indian caste system, described in bureaucratic and legal officialese as 'manual scavenging'. It is regarded to be so polluting that all, including even other dalit castes, avoid the touch of a manual scavenger. The situation of the manual scavengers had so outraged Gandhi's sensibilities, that he had responded by the personal gesture of insisting on cleaning his own toilet. But the system was sturdy, and survived not only his death, but continues even into the twenty-first century.

A law in 1993 [the Employment of Manual Scavengers and Construction of Dry Latrines (Prohibition) Act, 1993] declared the employment of scavengers or the construction of dry (non-flush) latrines an offence, punishable with imprisonment for upto one year and a fine of two thousand rupees. But the fate of this statute was similar to that of so many laws that are passed by Indian legislatures, which favour or protect the very poor and marginalized. These laws are rarely even acknowledged, let alone enforced. Narayanamma herself is an employee of the municipality district town of Anantpur in Andhra Pradesh. According to records of the state government, there are no dry latrines in the state of Andhra Pradesh. But in Anantpur we found that dry latrines were being operated by the local government itself, and cleaned by its employees. The irony of the government openly flouting its own laws is lost upon Narayanamma. Not only does the government maintain day latrines, in Anantpur as in many other parts of the country, it thinks nothing of employing as scavengers only members of designated castes who are traditionally assigned this responsibility.

In contrast to the polluting nature of her occupation, Narayanamma like most of her fellow workers, is always impeccably dressed, her saree spotless, her black hair oiled and neatly combed, and set off by white or orange flowers. Her home is spick and span, the floors and vessels bright and shining. There is a quiet assertion, of determined dignity amidst degradation, even a rebellion, in that cleanliness.

But Narayanamma is always chewing betel nut. The smell of the shit never leaves you, she says. Whatever you do, you smell it in your hair , your clothes, even in all that you eat. It is even worse when it rains, and the shit trickles through the basket onto your hair, face and shoulders. That's why we all eat so much betel nut, and, she confesses, drink quantities of country liquor. It is the only way we can live with the shame of our work.

Since no one's caste is written on the forehead, in the city most people from lower castes are able to gradually shed their caste identity and be liberated from it. But not the scavengers, who are always recognized because of their continued engagement with their despised profession. *Ai, municipality* come, clean this, is how most people call out to Narayanamma and her fellow workers when they walk down the road.

It is as though we do not have a name, she says. And often they cover their noses when we walk past, as though we smell. We have to wait until someone turns on a municipal tap, or works a hand-pump, when we want water, so that these are not polluted by our touch. In the tea-stalls, we do not sit with others on the benches; we squat on the ground separately. Until recently, there were separate broken teacups for us, which we washed ourselves and these were kept apart only for our use. This continues to be the practice in villages even in the periphery of Anantpur, as in many parts of the state.

Narayanamma was born in a village called Itukalapalli, into the untouchable caste of Madigas. Of her eleven brothers and sisters, only six survived. The family owned no land, and worked as agricultural workers, or 'coolies' as they were called. Her father also worked as a cobbler, and the members of their sub-caste, the Pakhis, the lowest of the low, were summoned regularly to dispose of human corpses and animal carcasses, and dig graveyards. Women also went for domestic work to the Reddy landlord households, and wage work was sometimes available for breaking stones in the Guntukal railway junction. But since everyone in the village relieved themselves in the fields, there was no need for any manual scavengers.

Narayanamma's mother died of tuberculosis when she was three, and so the little girl had to go along with her father, to the fields or railway lines. From about the age of seven, she too began to work at the sites. But when she was nearly twelve, her father also died. Her elder sister Pedakka, now decided that Narayanamma should be married. It was the only way that she could be protected. Pedakka had been married to Kadirappa, who worked as a manual scavenger along with his mother in the neighbouring municipal town of Anantpur. Kadirappa's mother died of a wasted liver because of the country liquor she drank to excess to overcome the shame of her vocation, and her employment in the municipality was passed on, a dubious legacy, to her daughter-in-law, Narayanamma's elder sister. Pedakka had been unable to give her husband any children. She thought perhaps Narayanamma would be more successful. So when her father died, Pedakka persuaded Kadirappa to marry her younger sister Narayanamma.

It was in the temple of the deity Pennaobelam, that thirteen-year-old Narayanamma was given to Pedakka's husband. He was more than thrice her age, but was kind to her. Their first-born was a boy whom they called Pennaobulesu, after the God who had blessed their union.

Some fifty families of the Pakhis, another scavenger caste from their village, were settled by the Anantpur municipality in low-lying land outside the periphery of the town. The colony was named Ambedkar Nagar. In time it became part of the town proper.

Meanwhile, Narayanamma's elder sister Pedakka grew increasingly frail. She too incessantly chewed betel nut and tobacco. A festering sore in her mouth eventually grew into a cancer that would be terminal. Initially, Narayanamma went along with the ailing Pedakka to the toilets, to help her out. But soon, her sister died. Narayanamma's first-born son was just two. Since then she had taken to her elder sister's occupation.

Recalling her early days at work, she said it was an on-going nightmare. Even as she entered the toilet she would feel sick, and this would worsen as she gathered the shit into the basket. The basket would weigh around ten kilograms, and she and the other women often felt weak and dizzy under its weight and stench. The men were once given gloves and wheel-barrows by the municipality as part of a government scheme to ease their burden. But the wheel-barrows were badly made, and so heavy to push, that the men went back to carrying the baskets of shit upon their heads. The gloves were much more useful, but why only the men got these, and that too only once, neither Narayanamma nor Kadirappa knew.

Their family grew steadily. After Pennaobulesu came a daughter and two sons. Kadirappa ensured that the children went to school. In the municipal schools of the town, there was less open discrimination and therefore they were able to get admission; Pennaobulesu completed high school.

When Pennaobulesu was in his late teens, Kadirappa suffered a stroke, which partially paralysed his left side. The sanitary inspector wanted him to retire prematurely, but Kadirappa pleaded to be allowed to continue, and with great effort moved his left arm to show how he was still capable and strong. His son would now accompany him and help him in his work. When Kadirappa finally retired five years ago, he tried hard to ensure that his son should get his job, despite his education. Somewhere in his mind the extreme social degradation connected with this job was compensated for by the economic security it offered. But Chief Minister N.T. Rama Rao had abolished hereditary rights over all municipal employment, and others of their caste competed for Kadirappa's position. The sanitary inspector demanded a bribe of 20,000 rupees to give their son the job, which they refused. If they had to raise and invest so much money, they might as well give the boy a chance in a more respected profession. The boy instead opened a tea-stall in Ambedkar Nagar itself. At least the residents of Ambedkar Nagar would not suffer the segregation seen in tea-stalls elsewhere. His tea-stall therefore does good business with the people who live in Ambedkar Nagar.

In 1998, a young man who introduced himself as Wilson Bezawada first visited them at their home in Ambedkar Nagar. I was born into the same community as you, he told them, I am also a Madiga, a Pakhi. I know your anguish and your shame, and I want to help you.

But, at that time, Narayanamma vociferously denied that any of them were engaged in manual scavenging, and shut the door on the face of the stranger Wilson. We do not know anything about the work that you speak about, she told him. It does not happen here.

The young man was determined to break what he knew was a conspiracy of silence. He returned to their home time and again. Narayanamma and her family, after a few visits, invited him into their home, and were entranced when they heard him speak. He did not work as a scavenger, yet he declared to all that he belonged to their community. There was so much anger, so much pain, when he spoke to them, but also so much pride.

He had grown up in the Kolar goldfields, Wilson told them. The goldmines, once owned by the British, were now run by the government. But long before his birth, his father had given up scavenging and become a gardener in Kolar. As a young man, Wilson offered to work as a church volunteer with boys who were school dropouts. From some of them, he learnt about practice of manual scavenging. He recalls he wept, when for the first time he saw what it meant to be a scavenger.

To work towards ending this inhuman practice became an obsession with him. He joined a seminary to become a priest, but soon left because its principal found his activism unacceptable in a man of God. He had taken photographs of dry latrines that were run in the church campus itself, watched, as he put it, by the Cross, and he urged the church authorities to stop this. He wanted them lead a campaign to end scavenging, but they refused to take up the issue. 'If we raise this problem, people will assume that all Christian converts are scavengers,' the church authorities tried to reason with him.

Wilson fought a long battle for over fifteen years right up to the year 2000, with the management of the government-owned Kolar goldfields. Once again, they refused to acknowledge that manual scavenging was being practiced within the precincts of the mine. He then filed a public interest suit in the courts, and was able to secure a court directive for the closure of dry latrines, and the employment of people from the Pakhi community in jobs other than scavenging. As a result, for the first time, members of his community were employed as welders, tanners, fitters, in 1988, although the dry latrines continued to be in use. But in 1998, when the regular sanitary workers went on strike, these boys were called back to work again as scavengers. Imagine our shame, these young men told Wilson. Our colleagues with whom we shared the factory floor until yesterday, would come to the toilets with a small pot of water, and we would arrive there with a broom and basket.

The boys' protests were of no avail. Nevertheless, it

further strengthened Wilson's resolve to build a powerful organization of people from scavenging castes, so that their voice and their struggles for dignity could no longer be ignored. It is only now in the year 2001 that the dry latrines in the Kolar goldfield are being shut, but this is not to belatedly restore dignity to those were worked to clean these latrines, but because the mine itself is being closed down.

Wilson's campaign to build an organization of scavengers has taken him to many towns in Karnataka and neighbouring Andhra Pradesh. He has sought more and more adherents for change from his community, mostly women, whom he found more resolute. It was this search which took him also to the threshold of Narayanamma.

She was also increasingly drawn to Wilson. A small but growing band, consisting mainly of women and youth of the community, has grown in Anantpur to oppose the practice of manual scavenging.

There are many in the community who are anguished by the daily shame of their work, and yet are unwilling to abandon it for the looming terror of unemployment. In the choice between dignity and security, most, initially, choose the latter. It is for Narayanamma and her friends to persuade them to risk the perils of unemployment, so that their children can grow up with dignity, with their heads held high.

On 18 April 2000 an organization called the Dalit Human Rights organized a national public hearing in Chennai on the problems of dalits in the country. Leading men and women in the areas of law and social activism were on the panel, including Justice Punnaiya, Justice Suresh, Ram Jethmalani, Mohini Giri and Justice Ramaswamy.

Among those who were invited to give evidence before this eminent panel was Narayanamma. It was only two years earlier that Narayanamma had denied to Wilson when he first knocked on her door, that she was employed in manual scavenging. Today, head held high with pride, eyes fierce with indignation, her hair oiled and adorned with flowers, dressed in her best saree, she spoke out to the world. She spoke of what she was utterly convinced must end.

Why should I feel shame that I do this work, she now asks. Those who make me do it have the real reason to be ashamed.

A BATTLE AGAINST FORGETTING
BHAGALPUR

In the district courts of Bhagalpur, a now familiar face is that of a gaunt-looking young woman called Malika Begum. She limps into the court room, unsteady on her one false leg. Barely lettered beyond what she learnt as a young girl in a *madrassa* and in the village primary school, she faces without flinching the cross-examination of a battery of lawyers employed by the thirty-three accused men. The cross-examination runs into several months at a stretch.

Each time, Malika stands steadfastly by her story, repeated hundreds of times, including before the Patna High Court and the judicial commission of enquiry established by the Bihar state government. It is a story of the most shocking brutality, of how her parents and fifty-nine other women, men and children, were hacked to death before her eyes during the infamous Bhagalpur riots in the sombre autumn of 1989.

It was the morning of 24 October 1989. The ancient town of Bhagalpur, spread out on the banks of the river Ganga in eastern Bihar, was seized by a frenzy that swept most of northern India at the time. The militant campaign to construct a Ram temple at precisely the spot where a

500-year old mosque stood at Ayodhya, had reached a decisive phase. Bricks stamped with the name of Ram were being collected from towns and villages across North India, consecrated by Vedic rituals, and paraded in aggressive, armed processions. And this precipitated a wave of sectarian conflict, the most extensive involving Hindus and Muslims since the bloody Partition of the country in 1947.

One of the most savage, widespread, and prolonged sectarian conflicts among the hundreds that convulsed the country in those fateful months, was fought out in the dusty streets and fields of the district of Bhagalpur. The town of Bhagalpur, with an uneasy minority of 30 per cent Muslims, mostly weavers of the famed Bhagalpur silk, became victims of communal hatred that followed the Ram Shila (bricks of Ram) procession of 24 October 1989. But what was singular about the violence in Bhagalpur, which continued unchecked for several weeks, was that the frenzy of killings and arson spread deep and far into the countryside. According to the judicial commission of enquiry set up by the Bihar government, as many as 250 villages were rocked by the brutal violence, apart from Bhagalpur town. The commission, which submitted its report in 1995, after collecting a prodigious amount of evidence, estimated that around 50,000 people were affected by the riots, through the destruction of their homes, shops or looms, or through loss of life or limb. More than 900 bodies, salvaged from wells, tanks, and fields, testified to the validity of the official figure of over 1200 deaths. The overwhelming majority of these were Muslim men, women and children. Among them were Malika's father and mother.

Even prior to the Ram Shila movement, the communal cauldron had begun to simmer in Bhagalpur. (The town had seen sectarian clashes in 1924, 1936, 1946 and 1967, but these had lasted for a few days, with limited impact, and had never spread beyond the town limits.) A few weeks earlier, a dispute had arisen about the route to be followed in the Vishahari Puja and Moharram processions, and the superintendent of police (SP) had reportedly made intemperate remarks against the Muslim community. His anti-crime drive was also directed at criminals of only one community, seven of whom were killed in police encounters.

On 24 October 1989, the atmosphere in the city was tense, vitiated by openly anti-Muslim slogans on the walls of the city and by pamphlets that were widely distributed. The organizers of the Ram Shila procession insisted on passing through some of the most crowded lanes of the city, inhabited predominantly by Muslims. The district magistrate reluctantly gave permission for the procession, subject to the conditions that weapons would not be carried and aggressive slogans not be raised. Both agreements were brazenly thwarted, once it set out.

Around noon, as the procession was passing by the Muslim school, stones and ·brickbats were reported to have been showered upon it from inside. There was no injury, but tension mounted feverishly, and the district magistrate ordered curfew. The truck laden with the consecrated Ram Shilas was turned back. A wave of violence started, as dispersing mobs set fire to Muslim shops and homes. The Muslims alleged that the attacks were carefully planned, as was evident by the fact that if

Hindu shopowners had Muslim tenants, the shops were looted but not burnt.

This was followed by large-scale arrests, mostly of Muslim men, even those who were respected within the community and had never been involved in any crime. Furthermore, violence accompanied the searches carried out in Muslim homes.

The flashpoint for the ensuing brutal violence was reached when a completely baseless rumour spread that the thousands of Hindu students living in lodges owned by Muslims in Bhagalpur town had been slaughtered. No one knows where the rumour originated, but it spread rapidly, like a dense and deadly fog of poisonous gas, which settled not only over the town but also surrounding villages. The district administration did nothing to quell the rumour.

Prime Minister Rajiv Gandhi visited Bhagalpur on 26 October 1989. He was met by a demonstration demanding the reinstatement of the SP Dwivedi, who had by then been summarily transferred by the state government for his openly partisan role after the outbreak of the riot two days earlier. Police constables and BJP party workers joined hands in the demonstration, and the prime minister succumbed and rescinded the transfer orders.

The rumours continued to multiply. It was stated that some Hindu students had been thrown into a well in Sanskrit College. When the stench from the well became overpowering, the rotting bodies were hauled out by the police and identified as being those of Muslim men, women and children. Despite this, the police did nothing to quell the earlier rumour, that the dead were Hindu students.

And so the madness, the killings and violence continued to spread uncontrolled, and with a terrible ferocity.

Malika was only seventeen years old at that time. She was the youngest of five brothers and sisters, all of whom were married. Her parents and she lived in a neighbourhood of about twenty-five Muslim dwellings, forming less than 10 per cent of the houses in village Chanderi. But this had never been a source of anxiety or insecurity because, in living memory, the communities had lived together in perfect harmony. The Muslims of the village were landowners, and relatively well-to-do. Malika's father also took on contracts for fruit orchards, in addition to cultivating fifteen to twenty bighas of rich alluvial agricultural land.

The village of Chanderi is only around ten kilometres from Bhagalpur town. It did not take long for the rumours of Hindu student boarders being massacred by the Muslims, to reach the village. Malika was petrified and bewildered to see the neighbours she had known since childhood, suddenly transformed into an angry, menacing, mob that surrounded their homes and demanded their blood.

It was Friday, 27 October 1989, and the men, though fearful, tried to make their way to the village mosque for namaz. But their path was blocked by the mob, now armed with daggers and trishuls, and swollen with men from neighbouring Hindu villages like Farakka and Mokalkah. Terrified, the Muslim population of over fifty women, children and men took refuge in Malika's grandfather, Minnat Mian's house, because of its tall and sturdy walls. They huddled together in the fragile safety that this house offered, as the mob fanned out and burned and looted Muslims homes, shops and places of worship.

Late in the afternoon, the district magistrate, accompanied by a force of the police and army, drove into the village. The mobs dispersed, and the district magistrate found the fear-stricken community taking refuge in the house, amidst the looting and arson. He left behind an army contingent under the leadership of Major Virk for their protection. Late that night, the inspector in-charge of the Sabour police station, under whose jurisdiction Chanderi village fell, came to the village and assured Major Virk that he and his men would protect the Muslims who were taking refuge in Minnat Mian's home. The soldiers took them at their word and prepared to leave, even as the hearts of the people inside the house went cold.

After that, it did not take long for the village mob to regroup. The slogans started again, and the walls and windows were struck by stones and missiles throughout the night. What was left of people's homes was set on fire, and the plunder gathered pace once again.

It was a cold and desolate dawn that greeted the terror-stricken group, inside the house. Malika's father and mother held her close and tried to comfort her with what words they could muster. The cries of the enraged mob were still audible, and it seemed far from being satiated.

The village headman and other elders gathered at the door. Do not fear, they called out to the people inside. Open the doors. We only want to search the house because we have heard reports that you have stockpiled arms. After that, we will escort you to Rajpur village, in which Muslims are in a majority, and you will be safe. Within the house, the older Muslims confabulated, and concluded that this was their best chance in the circumstances. The elders of the village would not lie. In any case, they would not harm women and small children.

And so, they opened the doors, and Malika filed out silently with the others. The mob had quietened down, and some men searched the house for weapons and bombs. They found none. The group began to walk across the village to the sanctuary of Rajpur. Armed villagers, many from Chanderi whom Malika recognized, lined the path on both sides, like a thick wall. Further back a posse of local policemen in uniform stood passively.

And then, suddenly, all went dark. Malika's brother, Ahmed, was one of the first to be hacked to pieces. Malika saw her father's neck being cut off from behind. Even her little cousins were not spared. She saw a small baby in her mother's arms being snatched and stabbed. In minutes, amidst chilling screams and slogans of Jai Bajrang Bali, some sixty-one women, men and children were dismembered by daggers and trishuls. Many of the bodies were thrown into a small village pond. Malika's leg was chopped off by a machete and she leaped into the pond. There was a macabre crush of maimed dead bodies around her. To this day she is haunted by the ghoulish memory of the body that was nearest her. It was that of her decapitated father, her beloved Abbu.

After a while—Malika does not know how long—the desperate wails and cries of terror were stilled. The mob slowly dispersed. A few of the men stayed back to cover the mutilated bodies in the pond with water hyacinth, so that passers-by would not be able to make out what lay below. In the pond's shallow, bloodied waters Malika lay completely inert. The wound where her leg had been chopped off bled and the pain was unbearable. But Malika knew that if she had a slender chance to survive, she must remain completely silent, completely still.

A few hours later hours later, when the sun was still overhead, Major Virk and his men drove through Chanderi village once again. They checked Minnat Mian's home, found no one there and feared the worst. They saw no bodies at first, but the ground drenched with fresh blood told its own tale.

As they were driving past the village pond, Malika spotted the major, and she seized her only chance. She pulled herself up, pushed aside the water hyacinth that covered her, and desperately screamed out to him. In amazement, the army convoy stopped in its tracks. Major Virk and his men pulled her out. With disbelief and horror, they found some fifteen more maimed corpses in the waters of the pond. At that point, Malika lost all consciousness.

When she came around, she found herself in a hospital bed in Mayagunj hospital of the district town of Bhagalpur. Around her were survivors of the brutal riots in neighbouring towns and villages of the district. She recalls in a dim haze a stream of powerful visitors and media-persons.

For Malika, this was a time of coming to terms with so many profound losses. Of her leg, of her parents, of much of her extended family, and of the community she had grown up with, and loved and trusted for all the seventeen years of her life. Fear, betrayal, sorrow, anger mingled and seized her.

Communal sentiments were palpable even in the hospital campus. The injured from the Muslim community felt unsafe, and most fled the hospital. Malika asked for a discharge.

She was eventually discharged from the government hospital after twenty-five days, and taken to the Barahpura relief camp. Stories of horror and brutality continued to pour in. Possibly, the most gruesome was from village Lugain, in which the local police assistant sub-inspector led a mob attack of 4,000 men on twenty-five Muslim households owing land. A hundred and eighty people were left dead. The bodies were first dumped into a pond, then into two wells. Later, they were taken out secretly and buried in three paddy fields, and cauliflower grown over them. Only when the bodies were ordered to be exhumed by a magistrate, did the world learn of the massacre.

Malika was haunted by her memories. She knew they would not leave her for as long as she lived. A Muslim business family took her into their home for a month to continue her treatment. Some people donated money for her to be fitted with an artificial foot in Jaipur. But after a week's stay there, she returned unattended, because the doctor there had gone out of station. A story about Malika was carried in the local press. The Governor, A.R. Kidwai, on the basis of this report, personally arranged for her to be fitted with an artificial foot at the Patna hospital.

It was on the orders of the High Court that Malika was admitted to the Danapur Military Hospital where she received treatment. While she was at the hospital, men from the Army, particularly Brigadier Mahinder Singh and Major Virk, took special care of Malika. Major Virk declared he was taking her as his daughter. He tried to persuade young soldiers under his command, who were bachelors, to accept her in marriage, since there was no one to look after her.

A Kashmiri soldier from Poonch district, Mohammed Taj 'Kashmiri', ultimately came forward to marry her. He was posted at that time in Ranchi, and she lived there with him for some months. He was later transferred to a non-family station. Mohammed then took Malika to meet his mother, living in their village Chunga, in Poonch. But she was unwilling to accept a bride who was not only disabled, but spoke a foreign tongue. Mohammed returned with Malika, and left her in Bhagalpur, where the state government gave her a small house, and over two lakh rupees as compensation for her parents' death.

Mohammed would return to meet Malika from time to time. On each visit, he would take a part of her compensation money. When there was hardly any money left with her, his visits became more infrequent, and slowly they stopped. Numerous letters to him, and to his regiment remained unanswered. So once again Malika found herself profoundly betrayed and desperately alone. He had left her with two children, a boy, Imtiaz, and a girl, Fatima.

In the immediate aftermath of the Bhagalpur riots, the police registered a large number of complaints of brutality and aggression by the Muslims. Ironically, they were reluctant to register those of Muslim survivors and eyewitnesses like Malika. This was despite the fact that the overwhelming majority of deaths and losses reported were of Muslims, and of the 250 villages affected, not more than five were those in which Hindus were in a minority and were attacked.

To take up the cause of people like Malika, a society of Muslim intellectuals and professionals, under the banner of the Millat Society, was formed. They led the relief work. Malika was taken by them to the Patna High Court where she told her story, and which she was to repeat again and again, hundreds of times over. The High Court directed that her complaint should also be registered against the assailants named by her, and be investigated by an officer not below the rank of a deputy superintendent of police. After investigation, a charge sheet was submitted against forty-one accused persons. These included the mukhia or village headman Mithu Yadav, and the sarpanch Dina Nath Sahay, who according to Malika had led the mob to Minnat Mian's house and persuaded them to open the doors.

Today, at the time of writing, more than eleven years after the massacre, one by one, in every case registered by Muslim survivors of the riots, the witnesses are turning hostile. Some have succumbed to fear, others to bribes. Many do not wish to reopen old wounds, as they rebuild their shattered lives.

Malika has received many threats to her life, to dissuade her from persisting with her case. There have also been substantial offers of money, which would have helped her survive her present destitution, and to bring up her two children.

But Malika remains one of the only witnesses who

continues to steadfastly stand by her statements. To succumb—she says—would be a betrayal of the memory of my father and mother. I can never forget or forgive people who killed even small babies, my little cousins. I will never give up my fight for justice, she adds fiercely.

Her cross-examination in the district and sessions court of Bhagalpur continued for over six months. Malika took little help from her lawyers. Standing firm on her artificial leg, she did not budge from her testimony as she took her place each day in the witness-box.

The courts have still not announced their judgement. And even when they do, it is likely that the battle will continue in higher courts for several more years.

The anguished memories of the massacre will remain with several generations of the families who lived through its horrors. But for the rest of Bhagalpur town, the district, the country, this memory it seems has faded, as though the terrible events of October and November 1989 never happened.

The battle this brave and frail woman fights is not only for justice against all odds. It is also a battle against forgetting.

Postscript: Barely days before this book went to print, the national daily, *The Hindu*, carried a small news item in its inner pages. On 8 February 2001, the additional district and sessions magistrate of Bhagalpur announced his judgement in the Chanderi massacre case. Of the forty-one accused, sixteen were convicted with rigorous life imprisonment. Twenty-two accused were acquitted for want of evidence, where three had died of natural causes in the course of the trial. Even though some of the most powerful leaders of the pogrom got away some justice had still come Malika's way.

A WOUNDED HEALER: LIFE WITH HIV

The deeply troubled state of Manipur in India's North East, has witnessed the fury of armed militant struggles and fratricidal tribal battles for decades. But in its spectacularly beautiful hills and valleys, thousands of young people began, from the late 1970s, to seek also a very different kind of solace. They would puncture their veins, injecting themselves with the heady but deadly heroin, and squander away their callow lives.

In a sense, these young people were trapped, both by the tragic alienation wrought by their history, and the accident of their geography. Manipur shares a long border with Myanmar, which, according to studies by the United States Drug Enforcement Agency, alone accounts for as much as 60 per cent of the world's supply of heroin. As the use of heroin spread like an epidemic in villages and towns across Manipur, parents responded with bewilderment and anguish, and state authorities were helpless.

Meanwhile, unseen, an even more deadly scourge gripped Manipur, to compound all its past tragedies. In February 1990, the first case of HIV was detected from the blood samples of injecting drug users. By July 1999, the cases of detected HIV positive persons had soared to a staggering 8,658, whereas 458 people were diagnosed with AIDS, and reported deaths from it stood at a tragic 110. However, this was only the proverbial tip of the iceberg, because the state and the people of Manipur had united in a conspiracy of silence and denial.

Virtually every other family in Manipur today has at least one member grappling, sometimes hopelessly, with the twin problems of HIV and drugs. But because of the stigma and shame associated with drug use and multiple sex, the families almost never openly speak of their suffering. Parents may talk at the most to their closest friends, of their children dealing with a 'cancer-like' disease. It is a code word that everyone understands, but the pretence is elaborately maintained. Some are in such despair about their children, who return repeatedly to drugs (with the risks of HIV infection), that they themselves plead with state officials to lock up their children in jails. One often finds young people fighting HIV and drugs behind jail walls. Undertrials are also forcibly tested for HIV.

The powerful church has fashioned its own response, most often moralistic and judgmental. One church group in the hill district of Churachandpur, with the consent of parents, places HIV drug users in fetters, and then houses them in small cages. The local community is then invited to sing hymns at the cages, and pray for the salvation of the youths, who most often scream and thrash around in the agony of drug denial. The underground, on its part, declares that it would kill HIV drug users, for they are shameful burdens on Manipuri society.

Amidst this culture of dense silence, shame and despair, it seemed like an act of madness that in September 1997 a signboard should have come up on a building in a busy street of Imphal, indicating the office of the Manipur Network of HIV Positive People (MNP+). Sick of hiding in the shadowy silences born of their stigma, a group of four HIV positive young men courageously decided to come out into the open. Thereby, they hoped to extend a hand to other people trapped in the desperate loneliness of their struggle to live with HIV. Today the network has more than eighty members, and many more have sought its help.

A founding member of this network is Deepak Kumar Singh Leimapokpam. The youngest of seven brothers and three sisters, he was born into a middle-class Meitei family in Imphal in 1968. His father was the manager of a local cinema house, and his mother sold clothes in the famed women's market. The family doted on him. He was the baby of the entire family, even his sister's son was older to him.

He was in the ninth standard when, unknown to his family, he experimented with drugs for the first time. He started by chewing tobacco, smoking cigarettes and popping pills. But his friends insisted that he was missing out on the real thing. In the United States, his friend's elder brother told him knowledgeably, everyone smoked hashish, opium, ganja, and then heroin. Excited and reckless, he decided to try heroin. The first time he smoked heroin, he vomited, had a heavy head, and vowed never to try it again. But in five months, he was fully hooked. He had just entered the tenth standard.

Money was never a problem for Deepak. He would easily collect money, in turn, from his many brothers and sisters, who never denied him anything he asked for. Occasionally, he would even steal from his father's trouser-pockets.

The family learnt the truth for the first time during the

Holi festival the following year. Eight friends had gathered for the revelries, and they raucously smoked and drank through the day, and raced noisily around the city in a jeep. Eventually, they were caught by the police, who searched them and their jeep and found them in possession of heroin. They were detained in the police lock-up for half a night. But because they were all very young, and from well-to-do homes, the police did not charge them with any offence. They only informed their families, who came one by one to the police station, to take their errant children home.

Deepak's family was devastated by the knowledge that their youngest and much-loved boy was addicted to drugs. His parents, and his older brothers and sisters, gathered to scold and counsel him. They locked him in a room for two weeks, then took pity on him and let him out. After all he was only a teenager. Many of us made mistakes when we were young, they reassured themselves. He would surely get out of it.

That winter, at Christmas, once again his friends went out to celebrate. This time, it was to Chandel district. They took with them fifteen grams of heroin. People there showed them how they could get much more of a 'kick' if they directly injected the drug into their veins. Deepak tried this, and soon it became an obsession with him. Syringes were hard to come by, so they attached ink-droppers filled with the drug to needles, and shared the needles between themselves.

Some months later, while making his bed, his sister discovered an ink-dropper syringe under his pillow. A family conference was hastily called once again. His brothers beat him in anger, and locked him up once again.

Deepak wept and said he wanted to leave the drug, but could not. Clearly, he needed help.

His brothers once again were supportive. After all, they told themselves once more, he was only a teenager. And since they did not want their neighbours and relatives to find out, they decided not to send him to an institution. Instead, they called a doctor home. The doctor was competent and he administered doses of a substitute drug to help him cope with the agony of withdrawal symptoms. This was his first experience of 'detoxification', and the withdrawal pain was excruciating, but his family was caring, and at the end of the treatment he found himself free.

But in just three weeks, he relapsed. Another ink-dropper syringe, another shared needle, another gathering of friends. Drugs were freely available, and Deepak found the temptation too great to resist.

His family found out again in four months. This time they were more harsh, but called the doctor home again for another 'detox'. This pattern was repeated four times over in the years that followed. Meanwhile, he missed classes, scraped through his examinations, and by cheating just about succeeded in graduating from college. By then his family had begun to lose hope.

He was closest to his mother and eldest sister, who would only cry and plead with him. His elder brother would say, now everybody knows. You have brought so much shame to the family. I wish you had died.

One by one, Deepak's brothers, started losing interest and faith in his recovery. In the end, only one brother, an engineer and a national football player, would continue to counsel and scold him, lock him up, beat him, bring in the doctor, and then also take food and Horlicks to his locked room. Deepak started selling his clothes and belongings to support his drug habit. His brothers, who indulgently used to buy him jeans and T-shirts, stopped all of this completely and gave him no money. But he still found ways to sell, pawn, steal, or beg to keep the drugs flowing into his veins.

One brother had years earlier found a government job in Delhi and married a woman from Bihar. He returned to Imphal to meet his family, from whom he had been estranged for many years. Hearing his story, he decided to take Deepak back with him to Delhi.

Deepak lived with his brother's family in Delhi for three years. His sister-in-law loved him like a son. His brother tried to persuade Deepak to join the Navy, but he refused. He admitted Deepak by turn to courses in shorthand, typing and computers. But he made little headway with them, and instead got entangled in a messy love affair with a Punjabi neighbour. After an unwanted pregnancy and abortion, he was forced to return in some disgrace to Imphal.

The very first day that he was back, Deepak relapsed into his old drug habit. Within a few months, it was the same as before. He began to sell his clothes, his tape-recorder and whatever he could lay his hands on. But this time he was acutely aware that he was letting his life slip out of his hands. He cried before his brothers, and said that he felt like an old man, weak and completely without energy. His brothers remained sullen and sceptical, but he pleaded with them. Lock me in a room if you like, or send me to jail, keep me in chains, do what you like, but I want to be free of drugs.

This time it was the brother just older to Deepak who came to his rescue. He took him to meet some of his own friends who had managed to kick the drug habit. These friends persuaded him to go to a rehabilitation centre. It is very different from a jail, they assured him. It is your only hope, they said.

Deepak was apprehensive but agreed to give it a try, and the next morning six friends arrived on their motorcycles, to extend solidarity and accompany him to Life Line Foundation, the rehabilitation centre. His brother's friends were right, it was not at all like a jail. The staff was kind and supportive, and gave him substitute drugs to cope with his wrenching withdrawal symptoms. For the first seven days, he was in a daze. He would fight, shout out, and writhe in pain. But he held tenaciously to his resolve. Although the substitute drug is normally administered for ten days, he chose to discontinue it in just seven. He gradually entered the routine of the centre— rising early, doing yoga, manual labour, counselling, group discussions.

There were sessions also to educate them about HIV and AIDS. Each time the subject was discussed, Deepak's fear knew no bounds. The risk behaviour that they described, multiple use of unsterilized needles to inject drugs, was what he had practised for years. Terrified, he would often leave the classroom at the mere mention of HIV. He did not want to know. And he did not want to die.

He continued at the centre for four and a half months. His brother paid all the charges. Day by day, he felt more and more rejuvenated. His resolve not to return to heroin strengthened, whatever happened. But popping pills? Maybe . . .

One day, with some other residents, Deepak stole some pills from the pharmacy and swallowed them at one go. He fell into a daze. The centre's staff was furious with him. Only one counsellor was different. He spoke to Deepak gently. He said, when a buffalo breaks down a fence to eat grass on the other side, would you be surprised? No. But if a buffalo bites a man, yes, surely you would be. What you did was not like a buffalo biting a man, it was only like a buffalo eating grass. I am not surprised at what you did. After all, we are only human beings!

Deepak felt very moved, and greatly drawn to this man, whose name was Vikram Nepram. He regards meeting him as a turning-point in his life. He feels it was fortunate he stole these tablets, because otherwise he might not have met the man who changed his life. Gently, Vikram introduced him to the twelve steps of Narcotics Anonymous. The first step was the acceptance that he had done something wrong, and a resolution to come out of it with the aid of God. If he crossed that hurdle, the rest of the steps would follow on their own.

When Deepak was finally discharged from the rehabilitation centre, he was warned that the most trying phase of his recovery still remained. This would be the phase outside the protective walls of the centre. His four and a half months there had given him all the tools that he required for his recovery, but the onus to use them well lay squarely with him. Vikram introduced him to a support group formed by Narcotics Anonymous, called the Wounded Healers' Group.

Their support, but most vitally his own inner resources were crucial in the most difficult months after his discharge. His family was entirely sceptical; they had seen him slip too often. If he asked them for money now, they refused. His friends and their parents avoided him. They saw him as a bad influence. He felt very hurt. But he persevered, and in the end proved them all wrong. When he did not suffer a relapse for two years, he found that he was able to regain slowly, but surely, the trust of his family and friends.

Meanwhile Deepak's nephews were reaching manhood, and he saw each of them making something of their lives. He felt the stab of being left behind. Taking a small loan from his brothers, he purchased cloth and started selling it on the Imphal market pavements. He felt proud when he began to bring a little money home.

The Life Line Foundation, impressed by his two years of abstinence, then made him a job offer for six months. In collaboration with the University of California and the Indian Council for Medical Research, they were conducting a study on the incidence of HIV infection among married, intravenous drug users. Deepak's task was to persuade these married couples, where at least one spouse had a history of intravenous drug use, to voluntarily agree to tests for HIV. Deepak succeeded in bringing forty couples to the testing laboratory.

One day, Deepak suddenly—as though on impulse—volunteered to have his own blood tested for HIV. The doctor gravely broke the news to him, that he had tested positive. Deepak received the information with calmness. All the injectible drug users whom he had known in the past, and who had agreed to be tested, had been found infected. So he had realized that his case could not be different. Deep within him, he already knew, and unconsciously, he had prepared himself.

The idea of MNP+ came to him when a friend from his earlier days came to him and wept, lonely and very frightened, because he and his wife had just discovered that they were both infected. So what? Deepak said to them bravely. It is not the end of the world. Do you know that I am also positive?

The idea that took germ in Deepak's heart that day was to form a mutual support group of people living with HIV, in Manipur. He first consulted his mentor Vikram, about this idea. Vikram was very encouraging and offered that Deepak start work in his own office.

Initially, there were many barriers, because of the culture of fear, stigma and silence that shrouded HIV. Would people be willing to come out into the open? The first problem was the underground, which threatened to shoot all people infected with HIV. Deepak contacted members of the underground and said to them, I have HIV. Why don't you put a bullet through my forehead? They were startled, and when Deepak spoke to them of his plans, they eventually agreed to let him go ahead.

He spoke to his family, who were afraid of the shame they would have to face by his public exposure. But he pleaded with them. Let me do something with my life. You know what I have gone through, as have all of you. It is only when I come out into the open that I can help others like me. They relented, and are today proud and happy about his work.

He spoke to many friends who were living with HIV to join him in founding the group. But most of them feared the shame and the glare of adverse publicity. The confidentiality of one young drug user had been broken by the doctors and the media, and after his exposure he had relapsed into his old drug habit. The same could happen to them.

Slowly, however, the group of four friends came together to constitute MNP+, the Manipur Network of HIV Positive People, on 7 September 1997. They hired a room, and outside it put up a large board, announcing that their organization was one of HIV positive people. Initially, their neighbours were outraged, and suspicious. They wondered what the young people visiting this organization did when they got together; they suspected them of assembling to take drugs.

Gradually things began to change. More people joined their group. For each of them, coming out into the open was terrifying, but it was also a liberation. It was a sense of escaping the isolation and loneliness of the dark, for the warmth and light of the air outside. Today, there are more than eighty members in MNP+. NGOs, the government, police and doctors have begun to refer people living with HIV to the group. People from the neighbourhood, even those without HIV, have overcome their suspicions, and instead have developed respect for the unlikely group of young people. Some have started encouraging and actively helping them in many ways.

Among those who initially joined MNP+, some have died, some have gone back into hiding, some have returned to drugs. But many like Deepak continue. The main idea in forming the group was to assist people living with HIV to overcome their fears, their discrimination, their loneliness, and their desolation. Clearly, the group has made a difference. Its members are mostly heartbreakingly young, but working with MNP+ enables them too to face the future with courage.

Deepak looks like any average young person in the Imphal Valley. His clothes are trendy, and he sports an earring in one ear. But when he speaks today, there is a difference. I have learnt that how long one lives is not so important, he says with conviction. What is important is how *well* one lives. I keep running these days, because there is so much to be done. I know I will die one day, like any of you. But somehow I know, deep in my heart, that when I ultimately die, I will not die of AIDS.

THE LAND OF JAGTU GOND

Everyday, as he returned to his hut from the fields, Jagtu Gond would pause for a few moments, his gaunt brown body glistening in the evening light, his eyes fierce and intense. Gazing at the stretch of lush green, thirty acres of some of the richest and most fertile land in the area, he would repeat passionately to himself—this is my land, and I will get it back at all costs.

The patwari records, however, did not bear out Jagtu's claim. The land stood in the name of Babulal Joshi, one of the most powerful politicians of the district. Babulal Joshi was a man of many facets—landlord, moneylender, forest contractor, PWD contractor, trader and politician. Every petty government functionary paid him obeisance. And, although he was himself never elected to the state legislative assembly or parliament because the seats were reserved for tribals, it was always his men who were put up and elected. They always acted on his bidding.

It was his land, Jagtu said. But the whole village believed that the only land Jagtu owned was one-quarter of an acre on which his mother, Suklia's hut stood, and where his animals were tied. The land had been in the name of Babulal Joshi for so long that people had forgotten that it had belonged to anyone else. But Jagtu could never forget. The land had belonged to his father,

Kondoo. And now, by all rights, it was his.

Kondoo Gond, his father. He could scarcely remember him, he had died when he was only a child. Jagtu's only memories of him were with a bottle of home-brewed liquor, sprawled out for days in a drunken stupor, and the bouts of madness in his last days.

But it was not always like this. In the long evenings, as they sat outside their hut and watched the setting sun, Jagtu's mother would tell him of how it had once been.

Jagtu's father, and his father before him, for as far back as they could remember, had owned the land which was now held by Babulal Joshi. At that time, the land did not have a tube well or tractor. The grain they sowed was coarse, and the techniques of cultivation were primitive. Even so, they grew enough to fill their stomachs, except in the lean summer months when their grain stores were exhausted. But even then they did not starve because of the forests. As long as they were there, no tribal needed to worry.

The first roads were built when she was a child, his mother recalled. They brought nothing but misery. With them came the patwari, the forest guards, the police constable, the excise inspector, and then the politician in khadi. With the roads came the outsider.

Before her own eyes she saw her whole world transformed. The outsider came to stay; he felled their forests and took away their women. He brought with him his trade. In the village markets, goods appeared which they had never dreamed existed. In exchange for salt, a basic necessity, and for cheap and garish trinkets, cosmetics and synthetic cloth that were so alluringly displayed in the village markets, the tribals would barter away all their produce. A kilogram of chirongi nuts or cashew nuts or tamarind would be purchased from the tribals in exchange for a kilogram of salt; this would then be sold for ten to fifteen times the price in the markets of Raipur and Bilaspur. Impoverished and dispossessed, the relentless lean months of the summer would stretch long as the tribals began to learn the agony of starvation. And the forests were no longer there to support them, as they had for generations past.

However, the trader would never let them starve. He was always there in their hour of need. But at a brutal price. He would lend them the money they needed to tide over their months of need, but at crippling rates of interest. The defenceless tribal found himself increasingly caught in the vice of indebtedness, from which he could not free himself. And before long, he would lose his jewellery, his livestock and finally his land to the moneylender. And so the outsider who came empty-handed to their villages, in time came to own most of the land and property in the region, and the tribal, once self-sufficient and proud, became landless, deprived and powerless.

So it was with Kondoo Gond. Suklia recalled that when she married Kondoo, Babulal already was the most powerful man in the region. Tribals from tens of miles all around trudged to his threshold in their season of want. He owned a jeep, at that time the ultimate symbol of wealth and power. The jeep had its other uses as well; she had seen the occasional tribal who failed to pay his dues dragged by the jeep in full view of the village. There was never any doubt about who was in command.

But it was rare to have to resort to such a naked

display of power. With the tribal, and his unshakable moral code, such terror tactics were mostly unnecessary. Suklia recalled how frequently Kondoo would, like so many others, borrow against his entire next crop. After that it was not necessary for the moneylender, Babulal or his henchmen to visit the village, his fields or his home even once. Kondoo would toil in his fields even harder than he had ever done when the grain was for his own kitchen. The crop was harvested, threshed, packed in gunny sacks. Kondoo would then spend the bus fare to Babulal's village to deliver the grain at his doorstep, keeping nothing behind in his own house. After that, of course, he would starve again, and before long he would be at Babulal's door for another loan.

The day had to come, as it had for so many others before him, when Babulal would send for Kondoo. Babulal said that Kondoo's loan had mounted so high that he would have to transfer his land to him. But there was one hurdle; a law had been passed that land could not be transferred from a tribal to a non-tribal without the permission of the collector. Babulal assured Kondoo this was a mere formality. He would simply have to stand before the collector and testify that he had received in cash the full value of his land.

Kondoo had always looked on Babulal with an amalgam of fear and awe. He would never have dreamed of speaking out against the Seth. But his land, his beloved land. How could he lose it? He begged and pleaded for time, another chance. He recklessly pledged all his other belongings, his labour and that of his whole family, his life itself. Babulal's voice acquired a new edge of steel. We'll go to Jagdalpur, to the collector's court the day after the next village haat-bazaar, he said coldly, make sure you are here.

It was Kondoo's first visit to Jagdalpur. He sat outside the imposing court of the collector, trembling. Though he mutely put his thumb impression on all the papers that Babulal placed before him, he secretly resolved that when he stood before the great officer, he would plead with him. Master, I don't want to lose my land. I know I have taken much money from the Seth, who has always shown so much kindness in hard times. I pledge that my family and I will work our whole lives to repay the loan. But we do not want to lose our land. Please, great master, our father and mother, give me one more chance.

Suklia recalled how he had summoned all his courage and strength in preparation for this moment. Kondoo, gentle Kondoo, who had never raised his voice even at a child, prepared to speak out before the great officer, in defiance of the Seth. Anxious and fearful, he trembled, as he waited that day in Jagdalpur for the moment when he would stand before the collector.

But that moment never came. He sat with tens of other litigants outside the collector's court, awaiting the announcement of his name by the court peon. But while the others went in one by one, his turn never arrived. He never understood what happened. Only years later, when his son Jagtu read the collector's orders did he realize what had transpired. The order said that despite notice Kondoo Gond failed to appear before the court, therefore, an ex-parte order was passed against him. Jagtu learned soon enough from his rounds of the courts that sometimes only a few rupees to the peon were enough to ensure that the illiterate litigant was not even summoned before the court.

From that day, said Suklia, began Jagtu's father's decline. It was not that he did not drink before. Like all other tribal men and women, he had always loved his drink. But now he no longer drank with joy, but with a lingering sadness, and a deep, quiet anguish. The bottle was rarely out of reach. In the last months madness overcame him. She recalled the long, expensive, nightmarish bus journeys to the district hospital at Jagdalpur, with little Jagtu beside her, and Kondoo's friends from the village for support. But all these efforts were hopeless; the doctors said that they could do nothing. Kondoo was a shell, a husk of his old self when he died.

Jagtu had always been different from his friends. Even in the ghotul, he rarely joined in the merriment of festivals, or the gossip and laughter of his friends. Always aloof, he spoke rarely and little. He had studied up to the fifth standard in the tumbledown primary school five kilometres from his village. The middle school was too far away, and he could see that his mother's daily struggle to fill their stomachs was becoming too arduous for her frail and aging body. He decided, rather than his mother, that he would not attend school any further. He began to work in the fields of the Seth, side by side with his mother.

But although he no longer went to school he had a strange hunger for the printed word. Children's textbooks, the odd government handouts that reached the village, the posters that appeared during election time, even the newspapers in which purchases made at the village haat-bazaar were wrapped, would be devoured with a passion.

When his mother first told him about his father's land, he resolved to get it back one day. The resolve endured and strengthened with the passing years, but he did not know how he could get his land back. He felt, however, that it would only be through the courts. He would trek there each day in the lean months of the year, when no work was available. While his friends amused themselves with the girls at the ghotul, he learnt about life in quite another environment, the courts. He saw it all, the unlettered litigants caught in a bewildering maze of petition-writers, touts, lawyers, peons, court-clerks, and magistrates, and the unhurried complex corridors of the law itself. I will get justice from this, he resolved. Even from this I will get justice.

The year was 1982. It was in the courts that Jagtu learned for the first time about the new law regarding tribal land. He quickly learned the section, 170B, introduced by the new legislation in the Madhya Pradesh Land Revenue Code. This radical piece of legislation provides that in all old cases of land transfer from a tribal to a non-tribal in which the tribal was defrauded or deprived in any way of his legal rights, the land would be restored to the tribal forthwith, without even the payment of any compensation. What is more, this progressive new section provides that the presumption of the court in all cases of land transfer from tribals to non-tribals would be that the tribal was the victim of fraud, and the burden of the proof was placed on the non-tribal to prove that there was no deceit or illegality in the transaction.

This was the law, Jagtu said, greatly excited, which he would use to get his land back.

He spoke of this new law to his wife Manglia that night. But she remained sceptical and unenthusiastic. The courts are not for the poor, she said. Have you known anyone to get justice from the courts? And the courts cost money. You, who eat what you earn each day after back-breaking work, and still remain hungry, how do you expect to find the money that you need to swim your way through the courts? And do you know who you are fighting against, the Seth, the great master? Will he let you survive if you raise your voice against him? Today we do not have much, but we are still living. If you succumb to this madness of the courts, we will be ruined. We will have nothing. Why can't you learn to be content, why can't you accept, why can't you be like the others?

Jagtu did not argue. But his mind was made up. He missed his mother greatly. She would have understood. But not Manglia. He had met Manglia in the annual spring festival of Marhai. That was three years ago, when his mother was still alive. According to the custom, he built his own separate hut at a small distance from his mother's and he set up home there, with his wife. His mother spoke much less those last months. Bent and wrinkled, she lived increasingly with her own thoughts. But in the evenings sometimes, she would sit with him as of old and watch the setting sun, and speak of gentle Kondoo, and of the land which was no longer theirs.

Yes, his mother would have understood. This he was sure of. But not Manglia.

Manglia wanted him to be like the others, but this he could never be. They were good men, he knew, indeed the best, the elders of his village. But they were too trusting, and too accepting. He would never be like them. He spoke of the new law, nonetheless, in the village. This is our chance for justice, he said passionately. After years of exploitation, this is our chance to get back from the outsider what is by right ours.

But nobody would listen, as he had half-expected. It was not just fear that made them unresponsive, although there were none in the village who were not in awe of the Seth. If people were convinced that their fight was righteous and just, then perhaps it might have been possible to persuade them to cast aside their fear and come together to struggle for what they believed was right.

But most did not even believe that this law was right. After all, they argued, as they had taken a loan from the Seth which they could not repay, he had a right to take away their land. And the younger ones said: the land was transferred by our father or grandfather who are no longer with us. We were still children then, or not even born yet. How can we stand before a court and say that the land was taken away by fraud when we have no way of being sure? Even if the court passes an order giving us our land, we will still refuse to accept it.

Impatient and tired of arguing, Jagtu withdrew once again into himself. But his mind was made up. He would not accept injustice. He would fight, fight until the end to get back what was his due.

Having gathered all the papers connected with the land, Jagtu stood outside the office of the sub-divisional magistrate. When shown inside, he did not betray the nervousness he felt standing before the table of the young officer. He spoke of his father's land, of the Seth Babulal, of the loan and of the Collector's court. He spoke of the new law, and of his resolve to get back his land which had been taken away by fraud.

The SDM said that they would institute a case in this court and assured him of justice. He also volunteered to

appoint a lawyer for him, under the legal aid programme
of the government. Struck by the unusual spirit of the boy,
and knowing the power that his opponent would wield,
the SDM sent for the best laywer who had argued before
his court, and made a personal request to him that he
accept the legal aid case.

Notices went out, and before the first hearing, Babulal
Joshi was in the office of the SDM. Dressed as always in
starched and spotless khadi, with a long red tilak on his
forehead, his hands folded, his voice soft but with an
unmistakable ring of authority, Babulal spoke to the SDM
of the case. He spoke of it disparagingly, and of the
obvious and outrageous canard, that a person of his
reputation and standing had engaged in any fraud. The
case would of course be dismissed, he said. The SDM was
polite but cold, and said that he could decide only in the
court. Babulal's visit was followed by a number of
telephone calls from people in influential places which the
SDM chose to ignore.

The hearing of the case started. The SDM received his
transfer orders. He had by then passed orders in a number
of cases in favour of tribals, and the non-tribals, alarmed,
had formed a 'Sangharsh Samiti' and collected a huge
body of funds to challenge his orders in superior courts.

The SDM was however determined to pass orders in
Jagtu's case before he handed over charge of his sub-
division. In order to give Babulal's lawyer no scope to
delay the case further, he decided he would keep himself
free for the date of the next hearing of the case.

Two days before the appointed date, Babulal Joshi
was again in the SDM's office, with folded hands. My
lawyer has gone out of station, on work, he said. I would

like a fresh date. The SDM refused, and pointed out that he had enough time to engage a fresh lawyer.

The morning of the case, a faint crackling phone-call came from Raipur. It was Babulal's lawyer. He said that the SDM could no longer hear the case, because he had obtained a stay order from the court of the Additional Commissioner.

How could he have obtained a stay order, the SDM asked when he had not even obtained copies of the proceedings of the court. The only ground for a stay order could be some prima-facie illegality in the court's proceedings. But for this, at least a copy of the proceedings should have been submitted before the higher court. I do not believe that you have obtained a stay order, the SDM said, and in any case, the stay order is not binding on me until I receive a copy of the order.

The lawyer panicked. He had sent the court's order staying further proceedings by post, but it would not reach until the following day. He pleaded with the SDM to wait only another day. The SDM refused.

Replacing the telephone the SDM passed an ex-parte order against Babulal Joshi, for absence despite valid notice. He called Jagtu and asked him to complete his evidence. He then drafted a lengthy and detailed order which he completed only late that night. Jagtu sat waiting outside the empty court. The copying clerk made out a copy of the order and the SDM then sent for Jagtu. Handing him the order, he said, at last your land is now truly yours.

Late the next morning, Jagtu was back in SDM's court. Indignant, he said, the tehsildar is refusing to give me possession of my land. It is my land, but he is still refusing. But by then the stay order from the court of the additional commissioner had arrived. Jagtu could not gain possession of his land.

Full of hope, Jagtu had believed that his fight was reaching its end. Little did he realize that his fight had only just begun.

Babulal filed an appeal against the order of the SDM in the court of the collector at Jagdalpur. Simultaneously, the hearing on the revision petition before the additional commissioner also continued. Jagtu found himself shuttling between Jagdalpur and Raipur, to attend the hearings. The collector confirmed the order of the SDM, but each hearing before the additional commissioner was concluded without any proceedings on the case. Armed with the collector's order, Jagtu once again went to the tehsildar to take possession of his land. But he maintained that the stay order of the additional commissioner was still in force, and therefore he could not transfer possession of the land to Jagtu.

The hearings were still proceeding before the additional commissioner when Babulal filed another revision application, this time in the court of the commissioner. So now he began shuttling between the courts of the additional commissioner and the commissioner in Raipur.

His lawyer stood by him all this while and accepted no money apart from what the government gave him for legal aid. But expenses still continued to mount, and one by one Jagtu sold away his goats and two cows, and the wood of the sal tree that stood outside their home.

Through all this, Manglia remained dispirited and pensive, but she never actively resisted Jagtu's efforts. She

knew that it would be of no avail. As one by one, the
animals went, she made no complaint. The greatest
wrench was the sal tree being cut down, because this was
the 'devgudi', the abode of the gods of the house. It bode
ill that the tree was cut down and sold. But Jagtu would
never listen.

One night two constables entered their hut, and
dragged Jagtu away to the police station, on the charge of
disturbing the peace. Manglia, now five months pregnant,
was distraught. She sold her last few pieces of silver
jewellery for the lawyer's fees, and to bail out Jagtu.
Another case started, this time in the tehsil court. So now
Jagtu spent his time rushing between the commissioner's
and additional commissioner's court in Raipur, and the
tehsildar's court.

If this was not enough, another notice arrived, this
time from Jabalpur. Babulal Joshi had filed yet another
petition, this time in the High Court of Jabalpur. For the
first time, Jagtu felt a little daunted. Jabalpur—he did not
even know where Jabalpur was. It was hundreds of miles
away, he was told. You had to catch a bus to Raipur, and
then after the long and dusty bus ride there, you had to
change two trains to get to Jabalpur. Until now he had not
even seen a train.

But he still had some money saved up from all he had
sold. His lawyer gave him a letter for a friend in Jabalpur,
who was practising in the High Court. The lawyer assured
Jagtu would help him. Jagtu then set off on his first
journey to Jabalpur.

After the first hearing, he returned to Raipur for the
case in the commissioner's court. Final orders were passed
by the commissioner, again in Jagtu's favour. But now he

could not get possession of his land because of the stay order from the High Court.

By the time he returned to his village, Manglia had given birth to a son. But Jagtu's joy on becoming a father was shortlived, for he could no longer evade the question of how he would pay to fight his case in the High Court.

Two days later, his mind was made up. All they owned now was their hut, and the small patch of land around it. He would sell this and go with his wife and son to Jabalpur. Somehow they would manage there and fight their case. Manglia heard Jagtu's decision without argument or comment. Only her eyes spoke, saying more than any words could. Nonetheless, she complied, and a week later Jagtu left his village, with his wife and infant son.

When the train pulled into Jabalpur station, Jagtu for the first time experienced the stirrings of panic. He had brought along his wife and son, but where would they go? How would they eat? When he had come alone, he had slept on an open pavement. But where could he take his family?

They passed the first two nights on the pavement. During the day, he would sit outside the lawyer's office, as his wife sat quietly at its gate, cradling their infant son. Food was expensive, and he already found their money slipping away.

There was no other way but to find work. After three days of searching, he found employment along with his wife on a construction site. His wife tied her son on her back as they worked, dust in their hair, in their mouths, and in their eyes.

They were given a small hut at the site itself, where

they stretched out that night, exhausted. The baby wept disconsolately, unable to sleep.

Jagtu was silent for a long time. Then at last he spoke, his voice choked with tears. Perhaps, Manglia, you were right, he said. It was my madness, nothing else, this obsession with the courts. What have I been able to give you? We have lost our home and hearth and everything we possessed. Even then, we are no closer to getting back the land that is ours. I don't know if we will ever succeed. Yes, perhaps you were right, it was only my madness. May be I, too, should have learnt like the others to accept, to be content.

Manglia's eyes changed. They burned with a passion that Jagtu had never seen before. No, Jagtu, no, she said. Don't change, don't ever change. Don't lose heart after having fought so long, so bravely and so hard. We will not give up, Jagtu. We will never give up. We will get back our land one day.

THE SECRET WOUNDS OF JATIN

Jatin was barely six years old when his father hung himself inside their home. Even at such a young age, he understood a little of why his father had sunk into such deep and impenetrable despair. It all started when his father's fingers grew stiff and bent, declaring to the world the dreaded secret of his having contracted leprosy.

Only a couple of generations earlier, in these Bhil tribal villages of the Nimar and Jhabua regions of western Madhya Pradesh, victims of leprosy would have been buried alive by the community. When Jatin's father was afflicted, there was still no treatment available for the disease in the villages. His mother shunned his father and left him and their young son for another man. No one allowed Jatin's father to come near them; he was not allowed to go to the village market, the bathing pond, to any place where people gathered, or to people's homes. Jatin recalls his father's utter desolation, as he was abandoned by all he knew, and loved.

There were many expenses after his father's death, with the funeral, repayment of old debts, and the bribe paid to the police as the suicide had become a police case. His father's land and bulls were sold, and his hut was demolished. Jatin's father's brother took him in as a servant, to graze his animals.

Three years passed, when one day someone noticed

the open sores on Jatin's feet. The villagers recognized these as unmistakable signs of leprosy. Jatin was gripped by a cold terror, as he saw his world collapsing in the same way as had his father's. His uncle turned him out of the house, and he had nowhere to go but the forest. Jatin would sleep on the tops of trees there, and beg in the village for food, which was thrown to him from a distance.

One day, the village patel took pity on the abandoned young boy. Go to Barwani, son, he advised Jatin. There is a large government hospital there, and I have heard that many patients of leprosy go there. You will surely find help there, son. Go to Barwani, and be cured.

That was how the young nine-year-old, most profoundly alone, set out from his village, turning his back on it forever. He trekked for several kilometres through the forests to reach the main road. There he was told that only the next morning would he be able to catch a bus to Barwani. The fare was two rupees, and that was the full measure of money that he carried, which the patel had given to him. He slept at the bus stop itself, and reached Barwani late the next afternoon.

Asking around, he somehow found his way to the sprawling district hospital. Timidly, he asked a ward boy where he should go first. He was told that the hospital had closed, and he should return the next morning. For the next six days, he hung about the hospital corridors, sleeping at night on the open pavements, with no money for food, but lacking the courage to beg in a strange town. No doctor was willing to attend to him. Eventually, a compounder took pity on him and examined him. He took samples of his skin, which confirmed that Jatin had leprosy. The compounder gave him some tablets, and asked him to return every month for his medicines. Faintly, Jatin asked him whether he could stay and eat at the hospital. He had nowhere to go, and had not eaten for six days.

The compounder told him that the hospital was not for people like him. But, he added, there was a place at the edge of the city not far from there, the Kodhi Bangla, where hundreds of people like him lived together. You will find a place there, he advised him.

The compounder gave him directions, but Jatin lost his way. He was distraught, when suddenly he saw a man begging, his body showing clear signs of the toll of advanced leprosy. Jatin recognized him as being from his village and the same man who had bought a bull from his father years earlier. Jatin ran up to him and told him his story. Do not worry, the man reassured the boy. You will stay with me from now on, at Kodhi Bangla.

Decades earlier, the former ruler of Barwani had constructed a small home at the edge of town for leprosy patients. This came to be known as Kodhi Bangla or literally 'home of lepers.' Abandoned by their families and communities in the same way as Jatin and his father had been, some three hundred leprosy patients of all ages had gathered over the years at Kodhi Bangla. They built tiny shacks and begged for a living.

The place was no different from ghettos of leprosy patients in towns and cities across the the country. The leprosy patients in Barwani lived as outcastes in their small, sunless and filthy refuge, denied even the most minimal human amenities, and shunned and despised by the residents. No one allowed them to come near, so giving them work was out of the question. They could be seen every morning in the market thoroughfares and outside places of worship, their wasted hand stumps, ridden with open, maggot- and fly-ridden sores, extended before passers-by, who felt repulsed.

As the disease advanced, unchecked by regular treatment, their limbs were ravaged and they awaited slow death. It was a community profoundly without hope, without a future. But it was still a community, better than their earlier desolation of absolute abandonment.

Into this community, Jatin was brought, and it is here that he grew to manhood. He took a wife from among the residents. Before long, his wife gave birth to a son. He named him Amit.

Since Amit's birth, Jatin was obsessed by a dream. He wanted that his son should never grow up with the stigma of being the child of a leper, the way he had been. Instead, he was determined to pay any price to ensure that he be restored with dignity to the world beyond Kodhi Bangla, free from the curse of leprosy. But for this to become possible, he recognized that he must first send his little boy to school.

But, at the time (only twenty years ago), this was an impossible dream for a leprosy patient. The prejudice against even children of leprosy patients was so savage and so rampant, that teachers refused to admit them to their schools. Jatin cleverly hid his deformed limbs, his face, fortunately, showed no sign of decay, and so he was able to admit Amit to a local government school. He drilled into the little boy the fact that he should never speak of his parents, nor where they live. And they were careful never to be seen with him.

But one day, walking back from school with his classmates, the child caught sight of his mother begging at a street corner. He ran to ask her for money to buy a sweet. His classmates saw him with her, and his secret was revealed. They taunted him and complained to the teacher, who was indignant and promptly removed his name from the rolls of the school.

But Jatin did not give up. He had heard that in the neighbouring district of Khandwa, Christian sisters ran a boarding school for tribal children. He had heard that they had no prejudice against leprosy. He wrapped his son's clothes in a bundle, and taking him by the hand, undertook the long bus ride to Khandwa. There he found the church, and made his way to the office of the Mother Superior. Jatin told her who he was, and of his dream to educate his son. The Mother said that the year's admissions were over, and that he should return some nine months later.

Jatin, however, was adamant. He declared quietly that he would not leave the convent premises until she agreed. He sat there outside her office for three days, in his own version of satyagraha or civil disobedience, until she finally relented. And that is how Amit started his schooling in the convent school that would be his home until he grew to manhood. Jatin and his wife sorely missed him—more so because being ostracized from the wider community (which is the fate of most leprosy patients with visible deformities), their son became their whole world. But Jatin was resolute that their shadow should not be allowed to fall on their son's future. They, therefore, never once went to see him.

Meanwhile, things began to change a little at Kodhi Bangla. One Catholic sister named Lellis began to visit them; she persuaded the inmates to give up drinking, and would gather the children to wash and feed them. An elderly communist school teacher, Trivedi, spoke to them of their rights, and of the government programme for social security pensions. He filled their forms, and some months later, miraculously, the postman began to arrive at the settlement, with money orders of small monthly pensions. Trivedi, would from time to time, organize the leprosy patients into processions to the office of the SDM (the seniormost local official) in the centre of the town, to demand basic facilities at Kodhi Bangla and timely payment of pension. The net result of these exertions was that one hand-pump appeared which provided them clean drinking water, but little else. The pensions continued, but erratically.

It was a few weeks after he had joined his first independent charge, in 1982, that the young SDM of Barwani heard a curiously dispirited clamour of slogans outside his office. He always made it a point to come out of his office to meet agitating demonstrators to understand their grievances, but the motley bedraggled group of wasted humanity that he encountered was quite unlike any that he had witnessed so far. The elderly communist repeated, as he had for years, their modest litany of demands. To their surprise, the SDM promised to visit their basti, to talk to them at length.

His visit a few days later left the SDM with a deep

sense of disquiet, even anguish. It was not just the sub-human degradation of the physical environment in which they subsisted, the closest to hell that he had known so far, that shook him. It was not even their wasted limbs and their raw, ulcerous sores. But it was their utterly crippled spirit, and the depths of their despair that pained him. They were victims of the scourge loathed and feared by humankind through centuries, which took its tragic toll not only of their limbs and faces, but also of the love and acceptance of those with whom they had until then shared their lives. As he spoke to Jatin and others and heard their stories, he understood a little of the magnitude and intensity of social prejudice against the disease, which was unchanged despite the medical advances of the twentieth century that had rendered the disease fully curable. He learnt how even today, patients of leprosy are abandoned and cast away by their families and by society, and are treated even worse than untouchables, because they are denied even the right to work.

It seemed to the young officer that there were few groups so completely banished from hope as the victims of leprosy. They were really 'the last in society'. He wondered whether he could help to build a life of dignity for these exiles. It was then that the dream of Ashagram, or a village of hope, took shape.

The SDM went again to the leprosy basti at Kodhi Bangla, and spoke to Jatin and others of his dream. They responded initially with bewilderment, then scepticism, then slowly with halting trust and hope.

He then called a meeting of citizens of the town to recruit their support. He realized that an enterprise of this kind was futile without strong, committed and sustained local public support. He was pained by the barely disguised hostility to the idea displayed by most of those whom he had invited to the meeting. Lepers beg because they are lazy and useless, they said; can you believe that people who have lived their lives as parasites will agree to give up begging and start earning their living? After heated debate, a respected elder citizen summarized their views with the comment, If you paint a donkey white, it cannot become a horse. The officer asked repeatedly, with considerable heat, how can you condemn a people before you have ever given them the smallest chance?

The meeting ended with no signs of citizen support for the enterprise. But in the week that followed, a small stream of citizens, a local respected businessman, a doctor running a successful private clinic, a public-spirited college lecturer, and of course the Catholic nun Sister Lellis and the communist, came to the SDM separately and pledged their individual support to the enterprise. He, immediately, constituted a public trust with them, and commenced work on the project.

The first step was to choose a site for the new village, Ashagram. The SDM asked the residents of Kodhi Bangla to select four or five representatives, and he took them in his jeep to scout for appropriate sites. After a few days, they chose a picturesque open space around low hills, with a panoramic view of the entire township.

The SDM applied immediately to the collector for allotment of the land for the project. To his surprise, the collector refused. But at this stage he could not give up, because Ashagram was no longer only his dream. He had initiated people exiled from hope into believing, hoping once again. He just could not let them down. Desperately, he searched for a solution. He found that the site selected for Ashagram was entirely government land, except for one acre, which was privately owned. He enquired and learnt that the owner was a childless widow Dayabai, who was too old to cultivate the land. He went to meet her, and requested that she donate the land for Ashagram, to which she readily agreed. He organized a public function, in which she was honoured as she handed over the papers for the land. The legal barrier to the building of Ashagram was now removed, and the officer decided that now that he had gained this small legal foothold on the site, he would encroach freely on all the surrounding government land to build the new settlement.

The only funds available were the extremely limited resources for rural housing, at that time restricted to Rs 1,500 per unit. The local businessman who had offered his services for this project, and who in time was to become its central volunteer, asked the SDM not to worry. He would make good all the materials and funds that fell short of the very modest government grant that was available.

The leprosy patients, the other citizens of Barwani and even the young officer watched incredulously as a graceful little colony rapidly took shape, in less than three months; neatly laid-out small cottages, a clinic, a workshed and a playground for children.

It is significant that then, and in subsequent years, almost all of Ashagram was built only by innovatively pooling government schemes, without the requirement of public donations.

Simultaneously, the officer spent a great deal of time discussing possible alternative vocations for the leprosy patients after they gave up begging. A few would service the new settlement itself, with milk, groceries and other utilities. For the others, a beginning was made with the setting up of a khadi spinning and carpet weaving workshed and looms, and tying up raw materials and marketing with the Khadi Board.

The day came when the leprosy patients were to move into their new homes. In a small quiet ceremony, in the presence of some senior officials of the district, and a band of Barwani residents, the new inhabitants of Ashagram began their new lives, leaving behind them the despair and degradation of their old habitation.

The SDM was transferred from Barwani only a few days later after a nine-month tenure. Before he left he spoke to the residents of Ashagram of the affection and respect that he had developed for them. He said that by resolutely abandoning begging forever, and by living with self-reliance and dignity, they must break down the scepticism of the residents of Barwani and show to the world that they were in no way less than anyone else.

He need not have worried. In the eighteen years of its existence, no resident of Ashagram has begged. They keep their little homes cleaner than any other basti of the town. They planted and tended fruit trees in their tiny garden patches, formerly completely barren, now lush green.

As they watched the malformed stumps of the Ashagram residents, earlier outstretched for alms, now struggling resolutely with their looms and thread, the scepticism and revulsion of the Barwani residents gradually transformed, first into a grudging respect, and then an almost total acceptance. Today no one hesitates to offer work to people from Ashagram, and Barwani residents proudly take visitors to see Ashagram as a local tourist attraction.

But the early months in the new settlement were not without problems. In the first week itself, even before the SDM was transferred, there was a rebellion in the local school. The teachers refused to admit the children of leprosy patients into their classrooms, and other parents threatened to withdraw their children from the school if these new children were admitted. Hours of pleading and rationalizing were to no avail, and in the end Sister Lellis took the children to a boarding school in another district, with instructions to both parents and children to strictly maintain their anonymity, in the way that Jatin had already done.

An unexpected problem arose within the new community when a dalit woman patient went to fill water from the only hand-pump at Ashagram. The other leprosy patients, mostly tribal and some caste Hindu people, angrily blocked her access to the pump. In the end, the SDM intervened, with a decree that the dalit woman leprosy patient had first right to the use of the hand-pump. If others had a problem with this, they would have to find some other source. There was sullen acceptance. But in time, the dalit woman volunteered her services as a nurse for the leprosy patients; she was given some non-formal training by the Catholic sisters, and is today revered by her community for her dedicated and daily service to them, healing their festering sores.

But, perhaps, the greatest lesson of community living came some months later. As the fame of Ashagram spread, many leprosy patients from the surrounding regions came to the new settlement in quest of hope. In time, a second enclave had to be built for the new residents. Among these was an elderly patient, blind, mute, paralyzed, his body covered with open festering sores and his own excreta in which he was forced to wallow. He was abandoned near Ashagram one evening by his family. Even the residents of Ashagram were completely repulsed by him and there was a near-rebellion when Sister Lellis insisted that he would stay at Ashagram. It was Sister Lellis herself who carried him to her jeep, drove him to Ashagram, and tenderly bathed, fed and cared for him, while others only watched.

But in the days that passed, from their extremely paltry belongings, someone came forward after a week with a blanket for him, then someone else with a torn coat, then other clothes, then an offer of food, and finally someone said that as he lived alone, he would be willing to take the old man into his house; Sister need no longer take the trouble to look after him. He died a few months later but with the quiet unspoken happiness of having shared the love of a large new family.

The SDM had been worried about how the project would survive and grow in his absence, after his transfer. What actually happened went well beyond his dreams. The members of the public trust for Ashagram came to give the project a major part of their daily lives. The central figure became a businessman, who handed over his trade to his brothers and sons, and took up this endeavour as his principal enterprise. He is a remarkable man, of deep compassion and extensive management skills, but very low profile, who shuns all publicity. The doctor migrated to the Gulf, but was replaced by another private practitioner who daily gives several hours of free service to Ashagram even today. The Sister was moved to another convent by her congregation, and left a vacuum difficult to fill, but other citizens took her place. Another dedicated nun, Sister Souzo, today lives in Ashagram and runs a primary school, in which every child begins their studies. There is now no resistance to children of Ashagram studying in any school or college in Barwani.

The surprise is that most subsequent sub-divisional officers also felt that they must contribute in some way to the growth and health of the project. For a few, it became a central concern, and in the process they felt themselves in some way permanently transformed.

The quest for viable and stable livelihoods for the Ashagram residents has continued. The Khadi Board was erratic in its supply of raw material, so this did not remain a reliable source of employment. The trust bought a horticultural farm, which has now begun to yield lucrative returns. Later, an experiment began with a massive community poultry farm, in which even the most aged and deformed of the residents found work. But, eventually, hordes of the chickens died following a series of epidemics and the farm closed down. Recently, the government sanctioned a major handmade paper plant. And, of course, with the breakdown of prejudice, a large number of Ashagram residents are finding work in Barwani town and the surrounding farms.

Five years after his transfer from Barwani, the first SDM returned to the district, now as collector. This time Ashagram took up a new agenda, to assist every handicapped person in the district with whatever surgery, aids and economic assistance that he or she may require to be enabled to lead of life of dignity and self-reliance. It turned out to be a monumental task, the numbers of such disabled persons in his district alone exceeding 10,000, several times more than what the prevailing statistics had estimated.

The trustees of Ashagram felt that it was an enormous unseen tragedy that in the absence of these small interventions by either the state or any people's organization, the handicapped in the vast countryside live out their days helplessly dragging themselves in the dust. They, therefore, resolved to add the physically handicapped to the agenda of Ashagram. The trustees built a hospital to provide on-going facilities for inexpensive surgery for the handicapped, and a workshop for making low-cost aids for them.

In recent years, Ashagram has reached out to one more group, which is as tragically stigmatized as leprosy patients. These are the mentally ill. This is the most solitary of all ailments, and the most misunderstood. An idealistic and compassionate young couple, a psychiatrist and clinical psychologist, gave up their lucrative careers overseas to live in a distant and culturally alien Ashagram. In five years they have reached out to more than six thousand mentally-ill patients, many of whom have received modern medicine for the first time. The journey of Ashagram continues.

Jatin today has seen fifty summers, and is a leader of the community, respected equally by residents of Ashagram and Barwani. He works hard as a security guard, and has saved money. Relatives from the village that had cast him and his father away with such inhumanity decades earlier now come to him for help and money, which he gives without hesitation or rancour. His greatest joy are his sons. Amit, a strapping young man, transformed by his years of convent schooling, is today himself employed as a teacher in a convent school. Jatin's younger son, born in Ashagram, has secured admission to an engineering college.

Like the wounds on Jatin's body, the aching wounds of his soul are at last almost healed.

WEATHERING THE STORM IN ERSAMA

Prashant was only in middle school when he returned home one day, to find the doors to the house locked. He kept knocking but no one responded. Panic-striken, he called his friends. They helped him squeeze into the house through a window. When his eyes got used to the light, he began to scream. His mother was dead hanging from a rope tied to the ceiling.

Prashant's father was a Bengali prawn fisherman in a village of coastal Orissa. Life had been uneventful until just two months earlier, when his mother had started weeping and fighting because his father had taken a mistress. After the dust settled a little, his mother's brothers took him, with his younger brother and sister, to their village Kalikuda, in the prosperous coastal district of Jagatsinghpur. Prashant's uncles were convinced that his father and mistress had killed his mother, and they filed a police complaint against him. He was jailed for two months. Prashant does not know what transpired then but his father was set free. The case lingered on in the courts, but in the end he learnt from his uncles that his father had been acquitted.

The wounded spirit of the three children slowly healed, with the love and acceptance they found in the home of their maternal uncles. Their mother's three brothers all lived together, with their wives and children, under the same roof. Prashant and his brother and sister were absorbed into the large and bustling joint family, as though they had been born into it.

With the passage of years, the horror of their mother's suicide and their father's alleged complicity in it, as well as his subsequent incarceration, slowly faded from the children's minds. They would not have believed that life could ever turn against them with the same brutality and heartlessness again. But it did. There were more storms to weather.

On 27 October 1999, seven years after his mother's suicide, Prashant had gone to the block headquarters of Ersama, a small town in coastal Orissa, some eighteen kilometres from his village, to spend the day with a friend. In the evening, a dark and menacing storm quickly gathered. Winds beat against the houses with a speed and fury that Prashant had never witnessed before. Heavy and incessant rain filled the darkness, ancient trees were uprooted and crashed to the earth. Screams rent the air as people and houses were swiftly washed away. The angry waters swirled into his friend's house, neck deep. The building was of brick and mortar and was strong enough to survive the devastation of the wind's velocity of 350 km per hour. But the cold terror of the family grew with the crashing of trees that had got uprooted and fallen on their house, some time in the middle of the night, damaging its roof and walls.

The crazed destruction wrought by the cyclone and the surge of the ocean continued for the next thirty-six hours, although wind speeds had reduced somewhat by the next morning. To escape the waters rising in the house, Prashant and his friend's family had taken refuge on the roof. Prashant will never forget the shock he experienced at his first glimpse of the devastation wrought by the supercyclone, in the grey light of the early morning. A raging, deadly, brown sheet of water covered everything as far as the eye could see; only fractured cement houses still stood in a few places. Bloated animal carcasses and human corpses floated in every direction. All round even huge old trees had fallen. Two coconut trees had fallen on their house roof, where they stood. This was a blessing in disguise, because the tender coconuts from the trees kept the trapped family from starving in the several days that followed.

For the next two days, Prashant sat huddled with his friend's family in the open on the rooftop. They froze in the cold and incessant rain; the rain water washed away Prashant's tears. The only thought that flashed through his mind was whether his family had survived the fury of the supercyclone. Was he to be bereaved once again?

Two days later—which seemed to Prashant like two years—the rain ceased and the rain waters slowly began to recede. Prashant was determined to seek out his family without further delay. But the situation was still dangerous, and his friend's family pleaded with Prashant to stay back a little while longer. But Prashant knew he had to go.

He equipped himself with a long, sturdy stick, and then started on his eighteen-kilometre expedition back to his village through the swollen flood waters. It was a journey he would never forget. He constantly had to use his stick to locate the road, to determine where the water was most shallow. At places it was waist deep, and progress was slow. At several points, he lost the road and had to swim. After some distance, he was relieved to find two friends of his uncle who were also returning to their village. They decided to move ahead together.

As they waded through the waters, the scenes they witnessed grew more and more macabre. They had to push away many human bodies—men, women, children—and carcasses of dogs, goats and cattle that the current swept against them as they moved ahead. In every village that they passed, they could barely see a house standing. Prashant now wept out loud and long. He was sure that his family could not have survived this catastrophe.

In this way—wading, groping, swimming, weeping— Prashant and his two companions made their way to their respective villages. On the way, one of the men found that his entire village was swept away. There was no sign of his home. But his wife and son had survived miraculously, and he found them in the cyclone shelter in Khuranta. But his heart could not bear the burden of all that he had witnessed that day. Two days later, he was to collapse of a heart attack.

Eventually, Prashant moved on alone. On reaching his own village, Kalikuda, sometime in the evening, he panicked further. Where their home once stood, there were only remnants of its roof. Some of their belongings were caught, mangled and twisted, in the branches of trees just visible above the dark waters. His heart went cold.

His last hope was a large cyclone shelter, which had been built only recently in the neighbouring village of Khuranta, by the International Red Cross. It was, indeed, one of the few cyclone shelters on the entire coastline in Orissa. When it was built, the Red Cross had asked for volunteers and young Prashant had given in his name. They had also been trained in first aid and rescue. If his family was alive, his only chance was to find them at this shelter.

Prashant finally reached the place, swimming desperately, and utterly weary. From a distance, he could see it crowded with people. Daring to hope, he pulled himself up on to it.

Among the first people he saw in the crowd was his maternal grandmother. Weak with hunger, she rushed to him, her hands outstretched, her eyes brimming. It was a miracle. They had long given him up for dead.

Quickly word spread and his extended family gathered around him, and hugged him tight in relief. Prashant anxiously scanned the motley, battered group. His brother and sister, his uncles and aunts, they all seemed to be there. No, his middle aunt was missing. With a sinking feeling, he asked about her. He was told that when the storm broke out, and they all had rushed to the safety of the cyclone shelter, she had stubbornly refused to abandon the eighteen heads of cattle that the joint family owned. She had drowned with them.

This aunt had been like a mother to him, and Prashant felt bereft once again.

By the next morning, as he took in the desperate situation in the shelter, he decided to get a grip over himself. He sensed a deathly grief settling upon the 2,500 strong crowd in the shelter, despite all the din and clamour. Eighty-six lives were lost in the village. All the ninety-six houses had been washed away. The village

population was predominantly Bengali immigrants
engaged in prawn cultivation, like Prashant's family. All
the prawn ponds had been submerged and destroyed. The
smell of shit and urine was all-pervasive. But even beyond
all this was the desperate hunger they now experienced. It
was their fourth day at the shelter. So far they had
survived on green coconuts, but there were too few to go
around such a tumult of people. There was rice stored in
the granaries of the one village merchant, but which had
also been submerged. Prashant was told that the villagers
had besieged him to give them the rice, but the merchant
had stubbornly refused, even though it had got soaked and
was rotting.

Prashant enquired about why the village head, the
elected panch, did not take matters in hand. But the panch
himself was distraught, having lost his wife in the cyclone.
Meanwhile, conditions deteriorated in the shelter. Almost
a dozen people, most of them old, had died of hunger,
cold, and probably, heartbreak.

Prashant, all of nineteen years, twice violently
bereaved in his short life, decided to step in as leader of his
village, if no one else did. He first organized a group of
youths and elders to jointly pressurize the merchant once
again to part with his rice. This time the delegation
succeeded and returned triumphantly, wading through the
receding waters with food for the entire shelter. No one
cared that the rice was already rotting. Branches from
fallen trees were gathered to light a reluctant and slow fire,
on which to cook the rice. For the first time in four days,
the survivors at the cyclone shelter were able to fill their
bellies. His next task was to organize a team of youth
volunteers—he described them in English as a task

force—to clean the shelter of shit, urine, vomit and floating carcasses, and to tend to the wounds and fractures of the many who had been injured.

On the fifth day, a military helicopter flew over the shelter and dropped some food parcels. It then did not return. The youth task force gathered empty utensils from the shelter. Then they deputed the children to lie in the sand left by the waters around the shelter with these vessels on their stomachs, to communicate to the passing helicopters that they were hungry. The message got through, and after that the helicopter made regular rounds of the shelter, airdropping food and other basic needs.

Volunteers began to stream in on foot and by boat, first of a local organization called Sarvodaya Mandal, followed shortly by the army—whom a young boy described as the 'Kargil people', after the battlefield of the recent war between India and Pakistan. They were joined by Prashant's youth group in clearing trees that blocked the roads, disposing of carcasses and tending to the sick.

Word spread that in the block headquarters of Ersama, the government and NGOs were distributing food and polythene sheets for temporary shelters. In the village, after the flood waters receded, its people had scoured the place for what might have survived of their belongings, and for any rotting food. Prashant instead, felt that they should avail of the relief being extended. He organized a team of men to go to Ersama to secure the share of food for the village.

This became a daily trek. The state authorities and NGOs distributed food only sufficient for one day at a time. After a fortnight, larger stocks were given for three days at a time, then for twenty days.

Prashant found that a large number of children had been orphaned. He brought them together and put up a polythene sheet shelter for them. Women were mobilized to look after them, while the men secured food and materials for the shelter.

Among the orphans was twelve-year-old Vasudeva, the eldest of six brothers and sisters. On the night of the cyclone, some hours before it broke, his disabled father heard the warning about it on the radio. Youth volunteers of the village who had been trained by the Red Cross persuaded the villagers to secure their lives in the cyclone shelter. But his father was among those who discounted the warnings. I have seen the floods in 1982, when the embankment of the river Dalaighai broke, he declared. Even that we had survived. Nothing will happen to us. But when the winds raged and the waters rose, his father's brother swam with Vasudeva and his two brothers to the safety of the shelter. His mother took his two sisters, then returned for her husband, father, and infant son. When they did not come the whole day—although a large number of dead bodies and unconscious survivors floated past the shelter—the twelve-year-old boy became desperate. He wanted to set out at once to search for them. His uncle's son helped by tying a rope to a standing tree, and then to another, enabling him to slowly approach their settlement. On reaching there, when Vasudeva found that nothing was left of his home, he knew the worst had happened.

It was children like Vasudeva and his siblings that Prashant took into his makeshift shelter. Heroically overcoming his grief, the twelve-year-old Vasudeva insisted on joining Prashant's youth task force, clearing roads, disposing bodies, and securing food for the village.

Some two weeks later, a young officer of the Indian Administrative Service arrived at their village, a trolley attached to his jeep loaded with a large tent and utensils. He said he wanted to set up a shelter for orphans and widows, and was looking for volunteers. The villagers led him to Prashant, whom, to his amazement, had already taken the children into his care. A shelter was set up called Mamata Gruha, and widows also were brought under its protection. An NGO took responsibility for the programme, which they called Sneha Abhiyan or Campaign of Love, and it appointed Prashant as a sneha karmi or community-care volunteer, in charge of the Mamata Gruha.

As the weeks passed, Prashant was quick to recognize that the women and children in the Mamata Gruha were sinking deeper and deeper in their grief. He persuaded the women to start working in the food-for-work programme started by the NGO, and for the children he organized sports events. He himself loved to play cricket, and so he organized cricket matches for children in the thirty-five Mamata Gruhas spread across the district. Prashant engaged, with other volunteers, in helping the widows and children to pick up the broken pieces of their lives. The initial government plan was to set up institutions for orphans and widows. However, this step has been successfully resisted, as it was felt that in such institutions, children would grow up without love, and the widows suffer from stigma and loneliness. Prashant's group believes orphans should be resettled in their own community itself, possibly in new foster families made up of childless widows and children without adult care.

It is six months after the devastation of the supercyclone. Vasudeva is firm that he does not want to be adopted or be taken care of, and stubbornly refuses all assistance and adult protection. It is I who will take care of my brothers and sisters, he declares with a resoluteness well beyond his years. I will rebuild my house where my parents' home stood. I will not go anywhere else. When I wake up every morning, I want to see the faces of people I know and have grown up with.

And as for Prashant, this time his wounded spirit has healed simply because he had no time to bother about his own pain. His handsome, youthful face is what the widows and orphaned children of his village seek out most in their darkest hour of grief.

THE HOME BENEATH THE RIVER

Two decades after he was uprooted from the land of his ancestors, Nanhe Ram still speaks little. Looking much older than his sixty years, he sits for long hours outside his dilapidated hut in the resettlement village of Aitma. He has no land, no cattle, no sons; his ageing wife labours all day in the forests or in the fields of the big farmers of the village, to keep the fires burning.

There is anguish but little recrimination, as he talks haltingly of the past. The first time they heard about the large dam that would submerge their village, he recalls, was when daily wages were twelve annas (which would probably be in the mid-1950s). Their village, as, indeed, the entire region, was hardly connected to the outside world, and until then they had encountered very few government officials. When men on bicycles, wearing trousers and shirts, rode into their villages to inform them about the dam, the tribal people living there had got scared and run away into the forests.

He did not know then that a gigantic thermal power complex was being planned in the neighbourhood of his village, at Korba, for which the two rivers that flowed there, the Hasdeo and Bango, were to be dammed. Fifty-nine tribal villages like his were to be submerged, twenty completely and the rest partially, along with 102 square kilometres of dense sal forest, to create a vast new reservoir of 213 square kilometres. No one consulted with the 2,721 families of these villages, condemned to become internal refugees in the cause of 'national development', about the project and how it would alter their lives so profoundly and irrevocably. Some 2,318 of these families, or an overwhelming 85 per cent, were tribals or dalits, who like Nanhe Ram were the least equipped because of their temperament, culture and lack of experience, to negotiate their new lives.

The survey work continued for six or seven years, and it was in 1961 that the first phase of the project, for the construction of the barrage and major canal was sanctioned. Nanhe recalls their fear and excitement when a small plane flew in as part of the on-going survey work. However, it was only a decade and a half later, in 1977, that the first settlement, Nanhe's village, was actually submerged. In the intervening years, construction continued apace, but no one from the government planned any steps for their rehabilitation or even as much as spoke with them about how they might rebuild their lives in the future. They were completely ignored.

In 1977, a few months before their homes were actually submerged, the farmers were packed into a truck and driven to the divisional headquarters of Bilaspur, located in the heart of the Chhatisgarh region of Madhya Pradesh. Nanhe recalls that they arrived at the imposing building housing the district office in the late afternoon, and were bundled into a courtyard. There they were addressed by an official, who informed them that their village would be lost to the dam reservoir in just a few months, during the next monsoon, and that the government was therefore paying them the first instalment of their compensation. For Nanhe, this was a niggardly Rs 540.

When their truck returned to their village, it was morning. The inhabitants found that the local revenue officer, the tehsildar, was waiting for them. The tehsildar wanted to recover the land revenue due from Nanhe out of this compensation amount. Nanhe lost Rs 300 to him, and the remaining Rs 240 also disappeared before long merely in day-to-day survival.

During the meeting at the district office, someone had timidly asked, But where are we to go when our village goes under in the next monsoon? The official had replied tersely, How do I know? Why don't you go to your relatives' homes? But, some weeks later, a band of activists held a series of meetings in their village. How can they ask you to go to the homes of your relatives, they thundered. Did your relatives build this dam? They organized demonstrations and rallies, in which many young tribals of the village also participated. Nanhe was confused and frightened, and he held himself aloof. Eventually, the government conceded that the tribal families that were being submerged would be given house-sites in a resettlement colony located in the forest uplands.

In the few months that remained, Nanhe made plans in his own way for the future. Where and how they would live, he did not know. He was worried first about his cow, whom they all loved. He knew that he would not be able to take care of her in the resettlement village, at a time when even keeping his wife and two daughters alive would be very hard. He also could not think of selling her, because she was like a member of the family. So he gave her to an Ahir cowherd, and promised to pay him Rs 150 each year for looking after her. Nanhe continued, despite all his subsequent tribulations, to save and send money for the upkeep of the cow for ten years, until the cow died.

Just a day before the monsoon broke, the trucks arrived. The people were given only a few hours to bundle their belongings into the trucks. They were then driven to the resettlement village, in which house plots of .05 acres each had been hurriedly cleared for them in the forest. The rains broke early, and Nanhe and his family spent the entire monsoon huddled with their few belongings under a mahua tree. In the dry spells, Nanhe struggled, trying to build a small hut, while his wife scoured the forests for food.

The remaining instalments of compensation were paid only fifteen years later, in 1992. Nanhe received a cheque of Rs 2,000, which he used to repay loans to the moneylender. Nanhe survived on occasional wage labour, but only barely. It was around then that for the first time, under pressure from activists, the government initiated a few livelihood programmes. Although the government has since spent some two crore rupees in the resettlement region in recent years to belatedly provide livelihoods to the displaced families, there has been little success. Fishing in the new reservoir is dominated by outside contractors. Forty lakh rupees were spent on a poultry farm, which ran for a few months, with twelve beneficiaries who were given 100 birds each. The birds suddenly died of some illness, and the farm closed down. The manager of the poultry farm departed after making a young tribal girl pregnant. This was the only productive outcome of the enterprise Amber charkhas or spinning looms were installed, but raw material supply and marketing were erratic. The looms provided wages in fits and starts, and that too of only one rupee a day.

The resettlement villages are at the periphery of the large artificial reservoir, connected by earth roads that get submerged after the rains each year. In these inaccessible, remote, artificial settlements, not only are jobs hard to come by but life is very hard in other ways as well. Schools, health centres, credit cooperatives and ration shops rarely function. If someone is seriously ill during the rainy months, the only way to reach a hospital is by undertaking a perilous journey of three hours on a small leaking dinghy.

Not surprisingly, of the 208 families that had been resettled in Aitma, only sixty remain. The rest have migrated, either to the forests as encroachers, or to the city slums, in desperate search of means for bare survival.

Nanhe is among the few who remain, because he had neither the strength, nor the will to struggle and to start life anew one more time. He sits quietly outside his hut for most of the day. But sometimes when he speaks, he says softly to anyone who is willing to hear. When I am on a boat, in the middle of the reservoir, and I know that hundreds of feet beneath me, at that very point, lie my village and my home and my fields, all of which are lost forever, it is then that my chest rips apart, and I cannot bear the pain . . .

THE SECOND RAPE

Long years after she had been traumatized by a gang rape, a humble, illiterate potter-woman, Bhanvari, continued her fight for justice in the courts. Living in a dusty village, Bhateri, very near Jaipur, hers is a story of exceptional courage and indomitability. When we visited her in the village, sixteen months after the gang rape, we found that she and her family were ostracized, and were living like pariahs. The villagers were openly hostile and mocked them, even as we asked them the way to her home. There sat Bhanvari, with her white-streaked hair and faded *lahanga*. Suffering had deeply furrowed her face, but it was clear that her spirit remained unbroken.

From her unfolded an extraordinary story of a woman's lone battle for justice.

It was almost ten years earlier, in the summer of 1984, on an off-day from the famine relief works, Bhanvari was sitting in the courtyard outside her small hut, moulding earthern pots. A woman, obviously from the town, came up to her and wanted to talk. She said her name was Roshan didi and she worked in a government department for women's welfare. She asked Bhanvari about herself, and Bhanvari obliged.

Bhanvari belonged to the *kumhar* or potter's caste.

They had two bighas of dry land, but it yielded little even after hard labour. Her husband Mohan, therefore, plied a cycle-rickshaw in Jaipur, and she worked in the famine relief works, whenever they were taken up. Roshan didi asked her about the wages they were getting there and about the measurement of the work completed. Finally, she asked whether Bhanvari could organize a meeting of other women of the village engaged in relief works. Bhanvari agreed and called a meeting, where Roshan didi explained to the women the wage rates prescribed by government for famine relief works, and how even illiterate women could easily measure the size of the trenches with their *odhnis*.

Roshan didi continued to visit the village in the weeks that followed and from time to time would organize more women's meetings. Bhanwari impressed her by her vocal participation in these meetings.

One day she asked Bhanvari whether she would like to work as a 'Saathin' (friend). She explained that government had started a new women's programme, in which the Saathin was responsible for bringing women of her village together to fight against injustice and social evils.

Bhanvari did not understand, and refused. The project director of the programme came to meet her, and she was nervous. But the project director did not give up. She persuaded Bhanvari's husband to visit them in Jaipur. On a day when he was plying his rickshaw in Jaipur, Mohan went across and met them. He was convinced that Bhanvari would not come to harm by working in the programme, and he agreed to work on her.

At the outset, Bhanvari was required to attend a three-week Saathins' training programme organized in a village near Jaipur. In this training programme, NGO and women officers from various parts of Rajasthan attempted to create an awareness among women about their situation, a consciousness that the oppression suffered by women is not god-given and irrevocable. Women had the choice of alternatives, to improve their status. The programme leaders also spoke of hygiene, child-rearing, the discrimination against girl children, and various social evils.

Initially, Bhanvari felt extremely homesick at the training camp, more so when her husband came to see her with their small children. He gently reassured her, that he was looking after the children in her absence, and she must go through with the training programme.

When she returned to her village, she began to organize meetings of women. The first issue she decided to take up, on the advice of Roshan didi, was that of wages in relief works. The women combined and confronted the time-keeper. Under pressure from them, he consented, although with bad grace, to pay them the prescribed wages.

Enthused by this success, Bhanvari then decided to fight for arrears of dues to them from their old wages. She spoke to the sarpanch, and then took Roshan didi with her to the naib-tehsildar, but to no avail. She then asked the women to organize a dharna at the tehsildar's office. The women reluctantly agreed, for the menfolk in the village were mocking them. In the first dharna, all that the women did, according to Bhanvari, was to eat their *roti pyaaz*, and simply return quietly. But Bhanvari persisted and kept on encouraging the women to struggle, and after nearly a year, they succeeded in getting their money.

These successes earned Bhanvari the grudging respect of some of the men in the village, and generated substantial support for her among the women, cutting across caste-groups.

The years that followed saw a remarkable change in Bhanvari. Like many other Saathins working in villages across Rajasthan, still steeped in their feudal past, she blossomed into a leader of change. She worked indefatigably to get sanctioned the pensions due to widows and the handicapped people in the villages. She organized women for vigilance against corruption in the public distribution system. She persuaded villagers to send their girls to school. An unusual campaign she started was to counter the local village prejudice against girls riding bicycles.

Then she moved into even more difficult areas. She organized women to protest against battering by their husbands. She would lead delegations of village women to the home of the offender until he was shamed into giving up wife-beating. With the help of Roshan didi and the project director, she organized legal and moral support to abandoned wives. She fought for government patta lands to be given in the name of the wife. She mobilized public opinion and fought against social evils rampant in Rajasthan villages such as child-marriage, death feasts, and social practices such as imposing second and third alliances outside marriage on unwilling women, for a consideration to the women's families.

The experience of Bhanvari was not unlike that of Saathins across the state of Rajasthan. Gradually, this unique programme gained increasing national and international attention, as observers marvelled how in village after village, in the feudal backwaters of Rajasthan, women had found a voice after centuries of silence, and that also through government intervention. Innumerable success stories were documented of rural women coming together under the leadership of the Saathins to break social bonds, and to fight oppression and social evils. Basking in the all-round admiration, this became the most prestigious programme of the state government. Collectors placed the programme high on their agenda, even though some expressed reservations, in private, about a programme that 'does nothing except break homes and families'. The chief minister went so far as to declare, 'What the Saathin says, can be taken as the chief minister's voice.'

But the utter fragility, the painful limitations of the social support to this singular government programme of women's empowerment, became clear in the events that followed. They were to lead up to the shameful brutalization of one of the women from Bhateri, who, it seems, had sparked off a whole process of social change.

Every year, during the festival of Aaakha Teej in Rajasthan, tens of thousands of infants and children are tied together for life in wedlock, in a bond beyond their understanding at that age. In 1992, the chief minister issued a public appeal against this practice, and the chief secretary directed district collectors to organize strong action to effectively prevent child-marriages.

Bhanvari learnt that several influential Gujjar families were insistent on organizing marriages of the children. (Gujjars are the dominant caste of her village, and comprise half the total number of households in the village.) Among them was Ramkaran Gujjar, a powerful panch of one of the village wards. Ramkaran Gujjar was determined that year to marry of his infant daughter who was less than one year old. Saathin Bhanvari tried to reason with him, but he was unmoved. She pleaded that if it was a question of money, he could place the money in a bank, and it would grow enormously by the time the child grew to be an adult. But he was adamant—it was a question of honour: 'mooch ka sawaal hai'.

Next she sought the assistance of Roshan didi to persuade Ramkaran Gujjar, but she also failed. Finally, the police was sent in by the district administration and they stopped the marriage. Nonetheless, the marriage did take place, clandestinely, the next morning and no subsequent police action was taken against the family. But the Gujjars were convinced that Bhanvari was responsible for the police coming into the village.

Thereupon, they resolved that Bhanvari should be punished. Retribution first came in the form of social boycott by the Gujjars. This persists until today. The Gujjars resolved not to buy any earthern pots from her. They refused to sell her family any milk. A tree on their land was cut down and their crop forcibly taken away. Threats were issued, and her husband was assaulted at home. For the sake of Bhanvari's security, he stopped plying his cycle-rickshaw in Jaipur. The family suffered acute insecurity and economic distress.

The climax came on 23 September 1992. According to Bhanvari, one evening as they were working in their fields, five men, including Ramkaran Gujjar, assaulted Mohan with lathis while he was relieving himself in a neighbouring field. He fell down screaming. Two men now pinned down Mohan, as he struggled. Another one held Bhanvari, while two others took turns to rape her.

Shocked and shattered, somehow Mohan and Bhanvari dragged themselves home. Because Bhanvari was trained as a Saathin, she knew she should not wash or change her clothes, as it would destroy evidence. Immediately, she wanted to report the case. She approached two Brahmin families for help, who in the past had been sympathetic to her. But they turned her away. Other supporters of Bhanvari in the village did the same. The last bus had left the village, and it was only the next morning that they could go to the police thana in Bassi.

There, also, they met with hostility, suspicion and humiliation before their complaint was registered, that too only after intervention by a project functionary. The only doctor at the Primary Health Centre was male and he refused to examine her, so she was referred to Jaipur. But in his referral slip, no mention was made of rape, only an examination to confirm the age of the complainant.

In Jaipur, the doctor refused to examine her without a magistrate's direction. The magistrate had to be contacted at home because by then it was evening, but he refused to pass any orders from his home. The police lodged them at the women's thana for the night. Bhanvari recalls with pain how even the woman constables taunted her through the night. The response of a senior district woman police officer the next day was no different.

It took the strenuous intervention of the additional director of the Women's Development Programme, a young and sensitive woman IAS officer, and a woman activist, to ensure that the medical examination was completed by the next evening, forty-eight hours after the incident. The magistrate had finally ordered only a 'general examination' and had cancelled the word 'rape' from the printed form. Even so the vaginal swab test was positive, and the report corroborated that there were injuries on Bhanvari's hands and legs.

Bhanvari and Mohan were then sent by truck to Bassi thana. It was past midnight when they reached; the policemen at the thana asked Bhanvari to leave her *lahanga* behind as evidence and return to the village with Mohan. Their pleas to let them spend the night at the thana were brusquely turned down. Taking her husband's blood-stained *saafa* to hide her nakedness she deposited her lahanga in the thana, and then the two wearily began the painful long trudge back to their village. After two or three kilometres, a truck stopped and gave them a lift to somewhere near their village.

It was dawn when they finally stumbled into their home. The children were unfed and crying disconsolately. The buffalo was bellowing because it had not been milked for two days. It was then that Bhanvari broke down.

The next morning, the deputy superintendent of police, accompanied by the director, Women's Development Programme, came to the village for further investigation. His manner and tone was one which Bhanvari was to experience again and again, with many others, in the long months that followed—insulting and demeaning, as though Bhanvari was a woman of loose character, the offender and not the victim. When she said she could swear that she was raped by touching *gangajal*, the DSP replied that *'isse gangajal hi jhoota ho jaayega'*, implying that her very protestations were suspect.

In the weeks and months that followed, Saathins and women's groups countrywide launched a concerted campaign for justice to Bhanvari. A massive rally of rural women, a month after the incident, in Jaipur was lathi-charged. In speech after speech, the anguished question that came up was: Why should the victim of rape have to prove that she is of good character? When suspected by Lord Ram, Seeta wanted to descend into the earth. From Seeta to Bhanvari has nothing changed in our society?

The government succumbed to mounting public opinion and media outrage by transferring the case from the local police firstly to the CID (Crime) and finally the CBI.

For Bhanvari and Mohan, the nightmare was not to end for a long time. Their social boycott by the village grew to include all caste-groups, including their own. No economic transactions, no social interchange. The police enquiries dragged on—the same insults, the same insinuations, repeated blood and semen samples.

Completely isolated and shunned in her village, Bhanvari was sustained most of all by the gentle support of her husband, who never once wavered. Since they had lost all their sources of livelihood, they were in penury, and it was other Saathins, women officers and women activists who took care of them. A rare relationship, as between sisters, developed between a few of the most sensitive women IAS officers and Bhanvari. And in these months of waiting and quiet struggle, the officers saw themselves getting transformed. Most of their colleagues felt, cynically, that they were too emotionally involved, only because they were women.

Finally, on 27 September 1993, the CBI confirmed a *prima-facie* case of gang rape against Bhanvari, and submitted a challaan in court. In November 1993 and January 1994, two of the accused were arrested. The district judge and then the Rajasthan High Court rejected applications for bail and anticipatory bail. In its significant judgment of 17 December 1993, the High Court confirmed that 'it is a case of gang-rape which was committed out of vengeance because Smt Bhanvari Devi made efforts to check child marriage of minor daughter of accused Ramkaran on "Akhateej".' In response to the judgment, finally the remaining three accused, who were absconding till then, surrendered before the court.

Despite all this, Bhanvari and her family continue to live isolated and shunned in their own village. For the village, nothing has changed. For them, the victim remains the transgressor.

DOOMED TO BONDAGE

It was in the weary winter of 1998 that Bilasini, with her husband and three children, left home. They joined the flood of around a hundred thousand people from the district of Bolangir, who each year are driven out of their villages, for anything between six to eight months, by desperate hunger and debt. On any day during the months between September and December, you can see them thronging the railway platforms and bus stations in the district, squatting in clusters, clinging tenuously to the poignantly tiny bundles of their belongings, and crying infants. Some eat the coarse rice and onions that they have packed, others chat in low voices. The children play in knots, excited by the colours and smells, the sights and sounds of the platform. Some of the women and men who travel out every year look a little more confident than the new migrants. Their numbers swell each year due to the continued grinding poverty in western Orissa. You can make out the first-time migrants most of all from their eyes, where fear and bewilderment struggle against a tentative hope.

Bilasini clearly was one of these first-timers; her infant son cradled in her arms, while her older daughter played with an end of her saree. Next to her sat silently the man to whom her father had given her in marriage some ten years earlier, Khirasindhu Bandhod, and his son by an earlier marriage, Sujan.

Life was hard for Bilasini for as long as she could remember. Her mother had died when she was only three years old, in Gandharabadha, a village neighbouring Patimal where she was now married. Her only sister had died earlier at birth. Deciding not to remarry, her father struggled to take care of the growing Bilasini himself. He owned barely half an acre of an upland field, on which he grew millets or traditional varieties of paddy. This kept them going for barely three months in the year. For the rest, he toiled in the fields of farmers in the canal regions, or cut wood to sell in the market. Bilasini never went to school, and she joined her father at work when she was ten years old.

He married her off to Khirasindhu Banchod when she was around fifteen. For the marriage expenses, her father sold half his tiny plot of land to his younger brother. Her dowry did not have as much as a bicycle and a watch, which even poor people usually succeeded in mustering. But there was a bit of gold jewellery for her nose and ears. Her husband was some two decades older than her. His first wife had been killed by a hyena, and she left behind two sons, one who was almost the age of Bilasini.

Her husband was not quite as impoverished as her father. Still, Bilasini had to toil all day, but she was well used to that. She worked beside her husband on their one-acre farmland. They grew vegetables behind their mud huts and kept two cows. She would cut wood, and set out early most mornings, trudging eight kilometres to the nearest market to sell firewood and milk.

It was for the expenses of their elder son's marriage that they took a loan of ten thousand rupees from the mahajan, a cloth merchant in Kantabhanji. The interest rate was 10 per cent per month. Hard as they tried hard to repay the loan, they just could not scrape together enough to repay even the interest, let alone the principal.

Ultimately, her husband decided that, like so many of their neighbours, the family must set out to find work in the brick kilns of Hyderabad. On the suggestion of the moneylender, they contacted one Bishna Sardar, a labour sub-contractor from Bharupilli village. The Sardar worked for a labour contractor named Biswanath Suna of village Bhanupali in Belapada block. The contractors were paid a commission by the kiln-owners on a pro-rata basis, for the number of migrant labourers that they managed to bring to the kiln. Apart from this commission, it is believed that the labour contractors were paid seven to ten rupees for every 1000 bricks manufactured by these labourers. The contractors also had close links with moneylenders of the region. They joined hands with the contractors and assisted them in the trafficking of labourers. Many of them were in debt to the money-lenders, who could prevail on them by 'persuading' them to migrate as a repayment of their bloated loans.

The Sardar agreed to advance Khirasindhu Rs 5,000 towards the repayment of his debt. The basic labour unit in the region is called a pathuria, comprising two adults, and one or more older children. Khirasindhu and Bilasini decided to take with them his younger son, Sujan, then sixteen years old, who would work with them as part of their pathuria. Besides, Bilasini had to take along with her their small son and daughter, because who would feed them while they were away?

The contractor's agent packed them into a truck one night, along with tens of other migrants from their village and the neighbouring countryside, and drove them to the railway station of Kantabhanji. There were hundreds more already gathered at the platform, all bound for the same destination. The agent bought railway tickets in bulk for the ragtag multitude of travellers.

They sat, bunched together on the platform the whole night, shivering a little in the cold. The sun climbed high the next day but their wait was still not over. It was only at noon that the train lumbered into the platform. The train, which is tied inextricably with the destinies of several thousands of dispossessed migrants of western Orissa, ironically, is called Samata Express, or a train dedicated to equity! Into its three unreserved compartments, several hundred migrant workers, clinging desperately to their children and their small cloth bundles, are pushed by the contractors' agents, during the five-minute halt at Kantabhanji station.

The compartments were already quite full, when the pressure of the crowd swept Bilasini and her family inside. More and more people were bundled in at subsequent stations. For the whole journey, there was just enough place to stand erect, amidst a crush of bodies, and with barely breathing space. Bilasini's arms ached as she clung to her two small, crying children. People from her fellow passengers' village were known to have suffocated to death during the journey. It was a huge relief when the train finally terminated at Waltaire station, some eighteen exhausting hours later.

There was not a drop of water, no food, along the way; the hundreds of passengers were faint as they emptied on to the platform. The contractor's agent gave them a loaf of bread for each family, and before long, they were again pushed into a train, this time to Hyderabad. Once more, a nightmare of a journey unfolded. Next, from the large and bustling railway junction at Hyderabad, they were packed into waiting trucks, which drove them quickly to the kilns located in the periphery of Hyderabad.

At the kiln, owned by one Anand Rao, they were given a few hundred unbaked bricks and polythene sheets, and were shown a site where they were to build their temporary dwellings. They were given just two days to clean and level the site, and build their shelters. For food, they were advanced Rs 100 per pathuria, to be cut from their earnings.

The rules were made amply clear: at no time, under no circumstances, were the members of any family permitted to leave the site together, either to make purchases, or for any other purpose. Each time people went outside the camp, they had to leave behind at the site some of their family members, as a kind of surety. Even if some workers did still manage to escape, there was another innovative, invisible barrier at the railway station. Ticket-sellers were bribed to refuse to sell tickets to people who appeared to be migrant workers, unless the labour contractors accompanied them. (Labour contractors confide that there are many costs in keeping the wheels of their trade in human traffic moving, and graft to railway-ticket contractors is only one of them. The labour and revenue officials, railway policemen, local police constables, all need to be paid regularly to enable the illegal movement of labour each year. The newest entrants in this list of people to be bribed are local 'youth clubs' in some villages, which have begun to demand that they be also appeased by contractors and kiln-owners with some share in the earnings. Otherwise, they threaten to complain to the authorities.)

The money that Bilasini and other workers received in the form of advance earnings every week at the kiln—Rs 100 per pathuria—was barely enough to buy *kanki* or broken rice, which in the village is fed only to chickens. Vegetables or dal were out of the question, but in order to disguise the taste of the kanki, they occasionally used chillies and onions, when they could afford them.

The fifteen-hour work-day began at dawn, and Bilasini with the other women would wake up at 3 a.m. to cook food for the families. The wages were Rs 60 for every thousand bricks. This was what one pathuria could complete on an average, in a fifteen-hour work-day. It amounted to a daily wage of merely Rs 20 per worker, for almost twice the length of a legal work-day, and which was far lower than the statutory minimum wage. It was also almost half of what the local Andhra workers demanded, explaining the contractors' preference for the impoverished and submissive work army that deluged the place from western Orissa each year. Bilasini's little ones played and cried in the dust, while Khirasindhu, Sujan and she worked without breaks, as hard as they possibly could. The loan had to be repaid, and they also had to eat in the year ahead.

Two months of toil passed, when one day in February 1999, Khirasindhu was incapacitated with severe stomach cramps. He was taken to a hospital by the kiln-owner Anand Rao, the labour contractor Bishwanath, and the munshi or accountant of the kiln, Suresh. On Bilasini's insistence, their son Sujan accompanied his father.

This was the last time that Bilasini saw her husband alive.

Two days later, the labour contractor tersely informed her that her husband had died after an operation. They did not take Bilasini to the hospital. Instead, her husband's body was stretched out on a waste patch of land near the kiln. There were two fresh long cuts in the region of his stomach and his upper limbs were swollen. Their son was nowhere to be found. She was told by the contractor that he had disappeared, and was lost in the teeming city of Hyderabad.

Bilasini was utterly distraught at this sudden and dramatic change in her situation. She refused to allow the body of her husband to be cremated until they found her son, and sat weeping quietly next to his rapidly rotting corpse. A day later, the kiln-owner and contractor said they could not locate the boy and forcibly took away the body for cremation, easily over-riding her fragile protest. For a few days, many brick-kiln workers refused to work, and set out to search for Sujan. But hunger and threats quelled this brief rebellion, and they returned to their labour at the kilns.

Bilasini could not comprehend what had happened. Passers-by whispered to her about the illegal trade in organs that thrived in the city, suggesting that her husband's kidneys had probably been stolen. The boy may have protested, therefore he was taken away. Only God knew where he was, and what had become of him.

Bilasini took advantage of the absence of the kiln-owner and contractor one day, and slipped away to find her way to a police station. She tried to explain her nightmare to the men in khaki, and pleaded with them to at least help her find her son. Bilasini did not understand what else transpired, but no case was even registered.

She was discovered when she returned to the kiln, and the kiln-owner was furious. She worked there for a few more days, but was so dispirited that in the end the kiln-owner paid her Rs 100 as wages, and the contractor bought her a return ticket home. In either arm she held one of her two remaining children, and because of this she decided to leave behind even her paltry belongings.

It was the same journey that she had undertaken less than three months before, except that this time her husband and teenaged son were not beside her, and the compartments were not so crowded. When she alighted at Kantabhanji station, she recognized some people from her village Patimal. They helped carry her children, as she slowly walked home.

The elders of her village heard her horror story, and took her to Turekala police station. She described once again the events that had led to her husband's death and son's disappearance, but they took no action. They suggested, instead, that she file a complaint with the labour officials. Accordingly, the village elders helped her file a complaint in the court of the sub-labour court at Titlagarh. The case remains unresolved to date. She also filed a complaint with the district collector, but this also yielded no result.

Some activists of a local NGO, Vikalpa, which works among migrant workers in Turekala and Bongamunda, came to know of Bilasini's story, and the injustice that she had suffered. The news was carried in some local newspapers, which briefly stirred the Titlagarh sub-labour court, but after a couple of hearings, things settled down once again, and were as before.

The NGO workers took Bilasini to the district collector. He said the best that he could do was to pay death compensation to Bilasini. But even in this, he was constrained because she had no death certificate. Even a copy of the police complaint in Hyderabad would have provided some evidence, he explained. But as things stood now, what was the proof that her husband was actually dead?

This collector was transferred and another took his place. He too said he was helpless to assist Bilasini but did not ask for a death certificate. However, he felt sorry for her, and sanctioned fifty kilograms of paddy and a saree from his discretionary Red Cross fund. He did not ask what she would eat and wear when this was over.

We spoke to her a year and a half after her husband's death and son's disappearance. Bilasini sat mute and still bewildered outside the plastered mud hut of a neighbour. Aged well beyond her years, a traditional, faded green saree covered her emaciated frame. Her hair was unkempt, her pierced ears and nose were without any ornaments, her tattooed arms were bare. Her naked three-year-old son, with a crusted wound on his forehead, clung to her. A slightly older daughter, in a faded torn frock stood silently beside her. Bilasini's brothers-in-law do not take care of her, nor give her a share in the land. Her father's twenty-five decimals of land is controlled by her cousins, who refuse to return this to her, even though she is her father's heir. Bilasini barely makes ends meet by cutting and selling firewood. Every other day she trudges eight kilometres to the market of Kantabhanji and back, to dispose it of at whatever price it may fetch.

Official records of the district of Bolangir claim that only 830 people migrated from there during the past year. A short drive of two and a half hours to the Kantabhanji railway station from the collector's office would reveal that on any one day, the actual numbers of migrants is several times the official figure for a whole year. Many migrants also travel on trucks and buses. But any official recognition of the real numbers would entail legal responsibility to protect the migrant workers. And so the government prefers not see! The official position is that the migrants are leaving the state of their own free will, without the intervention of middle-men, or loan advances.

There are laws to protect inter-state migrants, for their compulsory registration and rights. There are laws that ban bonded labour and child labour, and guarantee minimum wages. Land courts are expected to protect the land rights of women. Crores of rupees are spent each year by the government on elaborate schemes to combat poverty. There are government hospitals, and these are known to employ some of the country's best doctors. Trafficking in human organs and abduction are major crimes. Police stations, district collectors and courts exist to ensure justice is dispensed, particularly to the poor.

And yet, somehow, somewhere, all these seem to have just passed Bilasini by.

THE SEAL OF THE SARPANCH

In just one day, the world changed irrevocably for Pyarchand.

Many years earlier, Pyarchand had been driven out of his village Umarwas in Rajsamand district of central Rajasthan by nagging poverty and perpetual drought. He had a tiny piece of arid land that the government had allotted him, but someone had encroached on part of it and the rest yielded nothing. He tried his hand at a number of things; he worked on relief works, plied donkeys, sold cloth in village fairs, reared sheep, but nothing provided him enough to feed and clothe his family. His household grew steadily; it seemed that his four boys and three girls were always on the brink of hunger.

After years of hopeless toil, he believed that his tribulations had finally ended when his wife's brothers called him to live and work with them at Surat, a prosperous industrial town in the neighbouring state of Gujarat. He struggled in Surat again through many jobs, but soon ended up pushing a kerosene handcart around the dusty by-lanes of the city. He now was able to send money home every month for his family, and even set aside some savings. It was not a fortune, but he was content. Years passed, and his life settled firmly into its modest groove.

Pyarchand—Pyarji to his friends—therefore never

dreamed of what was in store for him. One day he
returned tired after a long day's work to his home in a
Surat slum and, to his surprise and alarm, he found
waiting for him two powerful men from his village in
Rajasthan—Nathulal Gujjar and Hari Singh Solanki.

On his many visits there, Pyarji had never dared to
speak to these men before. Being a humble dalit, Pyarji
knew—and accepted—his place in life. Then what were
these big men doing waiting at his doorstep?

They greeted him a little awkwardly, then quickly
came to the point. We have decided that you will stand for
elections as our village panchayat sarpanch or elected
village headman, they told him. Pyarji could not believe
his ears. How could he, a mere dalit Khatik, a humble
handcart kerosene hawker, aspire to become the village
sarpanch?

The problem, they confided to Pyarji, was that the
government had reserved the seat of the sarpanch in their
panchayat for scheduled castes. This made them ineligible
to contest the coming election. Instead, they had chosen
Pyarji for this responsibility. But why they had decided on
him they did not disclose.

Nain Singh Solanki, the thakur of the village,
unchallenged, feudal master despite four decades of
democracy, had consulted at length with his powerful
coterie about how best to deal with the seventy-third
constitutional amendment. This amendment, in 1995,
had resulted in the the position of the sarpanch being
reserved for scheduled castes, so none of the coterie
could stand for elections. But the former leaders could
not brook power slipping out of their hands, and even
less submit to the ignominy of an untouchable wielding

power in the panchayat. The dominant scheduled castes of the village were the Meghwals, who spurred by the power of numbers, were relatively assertive and confident. By contrast, there were only a few Khatik homes. The enquiries by Nain Singh and his band confirmed that the most timid, most submissive of the Khatik men was Pyarji. They learnt that he had migrated several years earlier to distant Surat, and earned his living as a kerosene hawker. Their best bet then was to install Pyarji as the new sarpanch, and to retain their traditional stranglehold through him. A delegation was deputed to go to Surat forthwith to persuade him to fight the election. There were only a few days left for the filing of nomination papers, therefore there was little time to lose.

Pyarji was utterly confounded. Even in his wildest imagination, he had not thought of himself as being the village headman. He protested, I have studied no further than class four. I do not have the faintest idea about how the panchayat works. My kerosene business here in Surat is very small, but it gives me a steady income, and it has taken me several years of struggle to finally settle down. Elections cost a lot of money, and I have no money to spend.

But the delegation sent by the thakur Nain Singh Solanki was not willing to listen to his objections. Each one of them was overruled. We will all help and guide you in your work, they assured Pyarji. The elections will cost you no money; we will give you all the money that you need.

How long was it possible for a humble, frightened, shrinking man to resist the importunate, powerful persons of his village? In just a day, he found himself on a jeep, driving back with them to Umarwas, clutching a small bundle with his life's savings, terrified, yet secretly even buoyant, about his future.

Pyarji remembers the election campaign only in a haze. Surrounded by the formidable Nain Singh and his gang, he was never called upon to speak. What he recalls are unending, dusty jeep rides followed by trails of excited children, a loudspeaker crackling with his name and appeals to vote for him, writing on the walls of huts and public buildings in the village, meetings at village squares and confabulations of caste panchayats. And on the last night, country liquor was distributed in every hamlet of the panchayat and there was drunkenness and revelry as if for a festival or wedding. When the votes finally were cast and counted, it was a decisive victory for Pyarji. He polled 966 votes, whereas his nearest rival brought in only 672 votes.

In the heady aftermath of the elections, Pyarji first tumbled down to earth when Lakshman Das gave him a bill of expenses that he claimed had been incurred for his election. Pyarji protested weakly that he had been assured that he would not have to bear these expenses. But, now no one remembered the assurance. He was told that Rs 35,000 had been spent on jeep hire charges, diesel, liquor. And, not to forget, there was Rs 2,400 for repayment of an old loan which Pyarji had taken to purchase sheep, so that he could qualify statutorily, as a candidate who had not defaulted on any bank loan. Pyarji had a total of Rs 18,000 saved up from all those years of lonely toil in Surat, and he now gave these up to Lakshman Das, his heart breaking. But even after this, Rs 17,000 remained.

To meet this, Lakshman Das offered to give him a loan. Pyarji agonized, how will I ever be able to repay this loan? But Lakshman Das reassured him that there are many ways to earn money in the panchayat, and it would not be long before Pyarji would be able to repay his loan, and even have money left over on the side. Pyarji after all was the sarpanch.

In the panchayat office, the secretary Gopilal Regar only gave Pyarji the seal of the sarpanch. He gave him no keys and no papers, and told him dismissively that he had no need for them. Whenever he was required to sign, Gopilal would show him where. The seal would give official sanction to all that Pyarji would sign.

Thus, began the stewardship of Pyarchand Khatik over the affairs of Umarwas panchayat. Through all his years of office, he always felt alone, as a dalit, and a timid, guileless simpleton, who had been catapulted into power that was ephemeral, and even perilous to him. The other panches or village panchayat members included Nain Singh himself, and other members of his upper caste coterie. A seat which was reserved for women, was filled by Lakshman Das's wife, who never once attended a panchayat meeting. Wherever her signatures were required, Lakshman Das simply put his own thumb impression on the papers.

Pyarji had studied up to class four, and he could sign his own name. Initially, he was content to sign, and more importantly, place his seal wherever he was told. He never drew the stipend officially sanctioned for him as a sarpanch; he was not even aware that he was entitled to it. But, from time to time, he was given a thousand rupees by Nain Singh or Lakshman Das for his 'expenses'. He was not unaware as time went on that money was being made illegally. But, rarely, when he summoned the courage to enquire about this, he was reminded roughly about repaying the 'loan' for expenses for his election. In time, when he showed further signs of restlessness, he was also given a tractor loan, as a collateral for which he sold his remaining assets in Surat. He was assured that this loan too would be repaid in the same way as his election expense 'loan'. Later, he was told he had defaulted on his tractor loan from the bank; the tractor was taken away, his collateral also flowed down the drain.

As months passed, and he signed and placed his seal on every paper peremptorily placed before him, it gradually dawned on him that a noose had put around his neck by the others, and it was gradually being tightened by them. Belatedly, he made feeble attempts to resist, but he was terrorized and threatened even more by the coterie. Isolated and frightened, he continued to do as he was told.

Then he heard of an organization which was fighting corruption in the region, called the Mazdoor Kisan Shakti Sangathan (MKSS). Its activists, renowned for the simplicity of their lifestyles and the courage of their struggles, lived and worked out of two huts in a neighbouring village called Devdoongri. To resist corruption in relief works and other development construction in the villages, the MKSS had organized a series of public hearings called *jun sunwais*. These meetings were feared, as before a large assembly of local villagers, the organization examined accounts and records connected with public expenditure in the villages, and detected several cases of corruption and malfeasance

Pyarji wanted the people of his village to know what was transpiring in the affairs of the panchayat. So secretly, he set out one night, unknown to the members of his panchayat, and made contact with the activists of the MKSS.

Initially, the activists were sceptical. It seemed to them a ploy by Pyarji to escape the consequences of his wanton acts of corruption. However, when the activists started visiting the villages of panchayat Umarwas to investigate, the real story slowly emerged. The first time a team of activists who had not met Pyarji visited his village, they enquired about the way to the house of the sarpanch. In the house, the scene they witnessed was a familiar one for rural Rajasthan. A man was regally seated on a string cot, whereas another was squatting humbly on his haunches on the floor, his hands abjectly folded. They presumed, naturally, that it was the sarpanch who would be seated on the string cot, but this turned out to be Nain Singh. The man squatting on the floor with hands folded was Pyarji, the sarpanch!

Further investigations by the activists yielded stories of spectacular corruption and misuse of office, which were stunning for their sheer brazenness and scale. Meanwhile, Pyarji persisted with his plea for a jun sunwai. The MKSS activists were caught in a moral dilemma, because they were certain that Pyarji could not also escape legal responsibility for the crimes. They explained all this to Pyarji, but he was steadfast in his demand for a public hearing. I know I am condemned in the eyes of the law, said Pyarji, but I want the people of the village to know who are the real thieves. However frightened he may have been—and as a humble dalit he was—Pyarji was clear that, above all, he wanted to restore his honour in the eyes of his village.

And so, two years after Pyarji's first contact with the MKSS, a jun sunwai was organized, in a village called Bori on 18 December 1999. However, in the interim, Pyarji already had paid the price for his assertion. Firstly, in May 1997, the other panches passed an official resolution of no-confidence against him. But only days before the meeting of panchayat to confirm this resolution, as required under the law, Nain Singh himself offered to Pyarji that he would bail him out. A bewildered Pyarji consented. Nain Singh organized a feast for the whole village, on which he spent Rs 10,000, which was then added to Pyarji's endless debt. On the day of the panchayat meeting, the motion fell because no one attended.

But the real blow fell almost a year later, in March 1998. A special audit by the district authorities had detected a cash advance of Rs 80,000 to the sarpanch without accompanying vouchers. Pyarji was suspended, and subsequently in July 1999, ignominiously dismissed from the post of the sarpanch. No tears were shed in the village, and the upper caste vice-sarpanch, also a member of Nain Singh's group, took over the stewardship of the panchayat. The jun sunwai became even more imperative for Pyarji, for the world to know the truth.

The meeting site for the jun sunwai in the December morning was bedecked and agog with excitement. Celebrities like writer-activist Arundhati Roy, and leading rights lawyer Prashant Bhushan, were among those who were present. But these names meant nothing to Pyarji and the villagers. The crowds poured in only because they wanted to share in the unravelling of the truth.

As village folk took courage and came forward to bear testimony and present evidence, the assembly of villagers was startled, then angered, and finally numbed, by the enormity of the crimes in the running of their panchayat. In village Dataniwas, a 'community centre' was constructed as an extension of the mansion owned by Nain Singh. In Asan village, again a 'community centre' was actually an extension to the sprawling house of ward panch Kamala Nath.

Equally shocking was the complete diversion to the rich of the welfare scheme for the landless and homeless, the Indira Awas, under which the government pays the entire cost of house construction for the poorest in the village who have no roof over their heads. Thirty Indira Awas houses for the homeless were sanctioned by the panchayat, of which not even one went to anyone who was remotely poor, let alone landless. The villagers gathered for the jun sunwai were outraged to learn that Nain Singh himself had filed a petition as one homeless person, and an Indira Awas dwelling was sanctioned for his wife, and also for his two brothers and three other relatives. One of the two brothers of Nain Singh took money twice in the name of two alleged wives; one of them was long dead, and the other just did not exist. Three other members of the panchayat, Moti Bai in the name of her son, Prabhu Das in the name of his wife, and Mithu Bai herself, became bogus beneficiaries, among others, of the Indira Awas scheme. In the same panchayat lived extremely poor landless Bhil tribals, who were not selected for Indira Awas houses, for which they were most clearly eligible. They were not even listed by the panchayat

as being officially below the poverty line, which would
have at least entitled them to benefits like subsidized food
grain.

The litany of deeds of shameless corruption did not
end there. A water channel drawn by the panchayat from
a tank constructed at the cost of Rs 2,50,000 was shown
on paper to irrigate the fields of Bansa farmers; in reality,
it irrigated only the fields of Nain Singh and his kinsfolk.
Central Rajasthan villagers build hathias or traditional
public platforms for village gatherings, by contributing
voluntary labour and resources. But thousands of rupees
were embezzled in Umarwas panchayat in the name of
building these platforms. Ghost wages were paid on the
basis of hundreds of false entries in the muster rolls to
nonexistent workers.

The outrage of the villagers and observers was
redoubled as incontrovertible proof of each of these
crimes, both copies of documents and oral evidence,
was presented before the assembled villagers. Nain
Singh was invited to present his defence; he claimed that
he had been manipulated by Pyarchand, the sarpanch,
but the people derisively shouted down this ridiculous
claim. The coterie still tried to lay all blame on the
dismissed sarpanch Pyarchand who had endorsed all
the works executed by his signature. But Pyarchand's
plea that he was manipulated and forced to submit
carried weight, especially because he did not seem to
have been a beneficiary in any of these misdemeanours.
The senior government officials, the tehsildar and
district collector, who were present at the public
hearing, had to admit openly that malfeasance on such
a big scale could not have been accomplished without

the active connivance of government and bank officials. The junior engineer, for instance, who ratifies the construction of an Indira Awas house at every stage, the block development officer who clears the list of names in the first place and the bank manager who is meant to identify an account-holder, ghost or real, to whom Indira Awas grants are released, were all clearly accomplices of the crimes.

And yet, even after the high-profile jun sunwai, on 7 January 2000, that followed the one in December, the district administration filed a complaint at the police station which listed the dalit sarpanch Pyarchand Khatik as the main accused. Several of the misdemeanours, for which others of the coterie were clearly implicated, were not even mentioned. Nain Singh and Kamala Nath were referred to as the co-accused to Pyarji, only for the community centres built as extensions to their houses. No government officials were listed in the police complaint.

After the filing of the police complaint, Pyarji lived each day in terror of his inevitable, and impending arrest. He was charged under sections 420, 409 and 120B of the Indian Penal Code, which are for grave offences, and the police was armed with a non-bailable warrant for his arrest. But even more than the police, he was in daily mortal fear of the wrath of Nain Singh and his henchmen.

Meanwhile, only weeks after the jun sunwai, fresh panchayat elections were held across the state of Rajasthan. Through the statutory revolving system of reservation of panchayat seats it has been ensured that Umarwas panchayat is no longer earmarked for a dalit. Lakshman Das, Nain Singh's closest ally, stood for the post of sarpanch. MKSS activists were among those who campaigned against Lakshman Das, because of his publicly affirmed record of corruption.

The margin between the two candidates was small, but in the end, it was Lakshman Das who was declared elected. He is now the new sarpanch of the panchayat.

A SHORTLIVED REVOLT

The arrival of a ponderous drilling rig in the village was announced by the excited clamour of children. Before long they were joined by the village men. Next the sarpanch came up. He firmly instructed the technicians about the proposed location of the new tube well. Slowly a murmur of dissent arose among a small group of young men who were standing at the edge of the gathering. There are already two hand-pumps in the main village, they said, and none in our chamar basti. Why should the third hand-pump not be in our settlement?

The sarpanch was outraged to hear the upstart chamars making such a demand, as were a group of high-caste men who had collected around him. An altercation followed, and the dissenters were properly thrashed, though no one was seriously injured. The rig technicians followed the directions of the sarpanch, and successfully struck water in the main village settlement, and went ahead to install a third tube well there.

It was the summer of 1991. The village fell in the Bundelkhand region of Madhya Pradesh, which has a long history of caste inequality and oppression. A dusty, thirty-kilometre ride from the district headquarters, it was agriculturally prosperous. Of the 136 households in the village, forty were of dalit castes. The majority of these were marginal farmers, who used diesel pumps to irrigate their tiny holdings with water from small seasonal streams meandering through the village. However, farming was supplemented by agricultural wage-labour and bidi-making. Of the remaining households, the dominant caste was Lodhi. The sarpanch also belonged to this caste. The others were mainly Thakurs and Brahmins.

The dispute regarding the location of the hand-pump resulted in the visible souring of relations between the people of the dalit basti and the rest of the village. A few days after the incident, the sarpanch called a panchayat of the upper-caste men of the village. The hand-pump episode was the first occasion on which the dalit boys had openly challenged the sarpanch and the established village authority. It was felt that if effective action was not taken against them at this stage, they would come together again and again to protest, and peace and order in the village would be permanently disturbed.

After considerable debate, a decision was taken that in order to teach them a lesson, in the forthcoming sowing season, no dalit farmer would be permitted passage through the fields of the upper-caste landowners to reach their fields, and none would engage them as wage-labour.

The boycott was unanimous and vigorous. The fields of most dalit farmers were not located on the roadside, which would have given them direct access. But this had never caused any problem in the past because for generations they had enjoyed unhampered right of way through the fields of the high-caste landholders. But in the face of the organized blockade, the dwellers of the dalit basti could clearly see the long shadow of want and deprivation fall over their settlement. The elders pleaded with the sarpanch and other village elders, *peeth par mariye, pet par nahin* (strike our backs if you want, but not our stomachs), but to no avail. A rebellious youth loaded a hired diesel pump on a bullock-cart and tried to ride through the upper-caste landowners' fields to his own. He was prevented from doing so by the landowner who told him that if the bullock-cart crossed through his field, the youth's corpse would return on it. The young man turned back glowering but crushed.

The young men then decided to seek the assistance of the district collector and superintendent of police (SP), both young officers and direct recruits, in the district headquarters. However, both these officers took no action, despite repeated visits and petitions. The dalits were then advised that the divisional commissioner would be more sympathetic, and so they met him at his office. He immediately instructed the SP to intervene, but the only action taken even after all this was the registration of cases under the preventive sections 107 and 116 of the Criminal Procedure Code, against *both* sides. The SDM repeatedly summoned both parties to his court, but passed no orders. The district executive and police together did nothing to intervene in the boycott, and to restore the traditional access of the dalit farmers to their fields. The sowing season passed, and these fields remained fallow.

It was but natural that tension between the two communities should continue to fester below the surface. A minor incident a few months later caused a fresh eruption. A dispute arose between the sarpanch's mother and a dalit woman over filling of water from the hand-pump; it ended in the sarpanch's mother smashing the earthen pot of the dalit woman and beating her up with a stick.

Because positions on both sides had by then hardened, the dalit community decided to lodge a complaint in the nearest police station, but again no action was taken. Two days later, two dalit men travelling by bus were arrested by the police. The dalits immediately suspected the hand of the sarpanch behind the incident. Promptly, all the dalit men of the community decided to go to the district headquarters to secure the release of the two who had been arrested. They were unsuccessful in their mission, but it ensured they were out of the village for three days and nights.

During this period, the upper-caste villagers decided to launch a wholesale social boycott and offensive against those living in the dalit basti. The *atta chakki* owners refused to grind their flour, the milkmen to sell them milk, the tea stalls to serve them tea; the grocery shops stopped all sales to them, and the shepherds refused to take their goats out for grazing. Men roamed the *basti* with lathis, smashing earthen pots and roof tiles of dalit homes. With the men away at the district headquarters, the women and children were alone in the village, and all they could do was to huddle in their homes, terrified, and without milk, food or water.

When the dalit men returned to their basti after three days, they were infuriated by the scene that they witnessed, and the fear that had built up. They resolved to force the district administration into action.

Their first halt was the police station, where the

station house officer refused to register their complaint. They then went to the district headquarters again, and met the DM and SP, but still no action was taken. By then, the sympathetic divisional commissioner had been transferred. As a final recourse, the young men decided to forcibly stop all traffic in protest, in the centre of the city. The DM and SP were forced to meet them once again, but this time on the public thoroughfare. In the pandemonium that ensued, the DM and SP were coerced into giving a public assurance that the dalits' complaints would be registered immediately, following which the agitation was withdrawn. Complaints against the sarpanch and other villagers were registered under Sections 341, 294, 506 and 323 of the Indian Penal Code.

However, the very next day, the police registered a large number of cases against the dalit men of the village, under Sections 341, 355, 294, 295A, 296 and 34 of the Indian Penal Code. The additional SP then himself visited the village and called a meeting of representatives of both communities. He warned them that now as heinous offences were registered against members of both communities, it would be best if they all consented to a compromise. He added that since complaints had already been registered, they could not formally be withdrawn, but if both parties agreed, no evidence would be brought forward by either side and the cases would eventually be closed.

The elders of the dalit community clearly saw that they were defeated, and reluctantly they gave their consent. Later, the elders repeatedly cautioned the young men to maintain restraint. Their grain stores were empty because they could not sow their last crop, they were without work, and the DM had ignored even their pleas to start public works on which they could find alternate employment. The social boycott by the rest of the village community persisted. Their abortive brief agitation to ensure police action against their tormenters had failed. And now that sowing time was drawing close once again, only one question haunted them. Would they be allowed to go to their fields to sow their crop this year, or would their paths be barred once again?

1984: STILL SEEKING JUSTICE

Two widows live out their days together in a humble, two-roomed tenement in a suburb of west Delhi. The older one, Harnam Kaur, is a sturdy seventy years, her daughter-in-law Daljit Kaur is almost three decades younger. They were both widowed in a single morning. The date was 1 November 1984.

For Harnam Kaur, the memories of Partition had never completely faded. She was born in a town called Bannu Guhaar in what is now Pakistan. She was the eldest of six sisters and brothers, and in 1946, when she was barely fifteen, she was married off to a young man who made his living through electrical repairs and fittings. A year later, with a four-month-old baby in her arms, she and her husband barely managed to escape alive across the line partitioning India. All that they had were the clothes on their backs.

Harnam Kaur recalls the terror of the Partition riots: the houses and shops set on fire all around, people being stabbed on the streets, the screams of women being raped, the scenes of plunder and the menacing sound of bullets resounding through the unending sleepless nights. It was the army that eventually rescued them and took them to the safety of a relief camp in Kurukshetra, in what was left of Punjab to India. Harnam Kaur hoped that she would never have to live through such fear and horror again. But that was not to be.

Harnam Kaur's family lived in the refugee camp for almost four years. Her husband's skills as an electrician came in handy and enabled them to restart life once again. They moved from the camp to a small, rented house in the city of Ambala, where her husband found work in people's homes, schools, and sometimes with contractors. What he earned could keep the growing family going. She had four children by the time they moved a few years later to Anand Parbat in Delhi. Four more children were to follow. Among her eight children, four were boys.

The boys, except one who worked in a factory, all learnt their father's trade. One by one the children were married off, and Harnam Kaur was content that she had fulfilled her duties as expected, according to the cycle of life that she held sacred.

Her husband had had a stroke, which partially paralysed one side of his body. He had moved in with two sons, both electricians, whereas he himself now ran a general store in Trilokpuri, a resettlement colony on the far side of the river Jamuna. Harnam Kaur lived with her eldest son in their home in Anand Parbat.

At Partition, the Sikh community comprised only 1.2 per cent of the total population of the city of Delhi. By 1984, their population had grown to around 7.5 per cent (an estimated 5,00,000 people), as against a dominant 83 per cent Hindus. Many of the Sikhs had made fortunes in Delhi and lived in garish and opulent homes in the city's up-market localities. Other working-class Sikhs, like Harnam Kaur's extended family, lived in small tenements, in colonies like Anand Parbat and Trilokpuri on the outskirts. These settlements had both Sikhs and Hindus.

But despite growing unrest and militancy in Punjab, there was no history of violence by the dominant Hindu community against the Sikhs, who were generally respected for their industry, enterprise and patriotism. The majority of Hindus in fact regarded the Sikhs as virtually an extension of the Hindu community.

This altered dramatically during the mid-1980s, as politicians in both communities fostered distrust and division. The climax was reached in the summer of 1984, when Prime Minister Indira Gandhi used the army in a major military operation against the most sacred Sikh shrine, the Golden Temple in Amritsar, where Sikh militants were hiding. Sikhs everywhere felt violated and betrayed by the sacrilege committed by their own government, and in a mad, reckless act of vengeance, Mrs Gandhi's own trusted Sikh bodyguards turned on her and assassinated her in the morning of 31 October 1984.

Late that afternoon, her son Rajiv Gandhi, until recently an airline pilot, was sworn in as prime minister. By evening, reports of violence against Sikhs, countrywide, began pouring in. One of the first colonies to be hit by the violence against the Sikh community in Delhi was Trilokpuri, where Daljit lived with her husband and father-in-law. By the next morning, many parts of the country were simultaneously engulfed in possibly the most widespread communal violence since Partition, nearly four decades earlier.

No one knows how exactly the violence started in Trilokpuri. According to an inquiry conducted later that year by the country's two major civil liberties organizations, the People's Union of Democratic Rights and the People's Union for Civil Liberties, the beginnings

of the tragedy could be traced to the night of Indira
Gandhi's assassination, when the ruling Congress (I)
counsellor Ashok Kumar, a doctor who runs a clinic in
Kalyanpuri, one kilometre from Trilokpuri, held a
meeting. In it he alleged that Sikhs were distributing
sweets and lighting lamps to celebrate Indira Gandhi's
death. These were the rumours that were circulating
across the country. He then led an angry mob to the local
gurudwara, a modest Sikh shrine, which was set on fire.

Through the night, armed young men arrived in tempo
vans, scooters, motorcycles and trucks. By morning, they
were on the streets everywhere, shouting slogans,
brandishing staffs, trishuls, iron rods, swords and daggers.
Some of the men were neighbours whom they could
recognize, but a large number were residents of urban
villages in the vicinity of the colony.

Daljit Kaur's father-in-law, her husband and her
unmarried younger brother-in-law, hid under quilts in one
of the rooms, terrified. However, as the mobs drew closer,
banging on doors and pulling out the men amidst the
screams of children and women, Daljit Kaur took them
furtively from a rear door to a shaded, open plot on a side
lane some distance away from their home. She hoped they
would be safe there. She waited with them for a while,
then stealthily returned home, to smuggle them some food
and water. By the time she went back with something for
them, all the these three men in her family were dead. They
had been first battered with iron rods and sticks, then
brutally burnt alive.

Dry-eyed, she sank stunned beside the half-burnt
bodies of the three of them. Around her, there were flames
and smoke everywhere, as houses, shops, vehicles and

men were being set on fire. One car was set alight with a live man locked inside. Some houses were doused with kerosene, diesel and petrol and set on fire, the doors bolted to prevent anyone from escaping the flames. There were shopkeepers who kept up the supply of kerosene for the rampaging mobs. Even some women joined in the looting of shops and homes. The odd police jeeps patrolling watched tolerantly from a distance. Occasionally, the men in khaki were themselves seen helping the mobs by emptying out diesel and petrol from their own police jeeps.

Daljit watched helplessly, as her own house was systematically looted, then set on fire. She later learnt that their general store had also been reduced to ashes.

Her thoughts at that time centred on the bodies of the three family members that were lying there near her, even as a mad frenzy raged all round. At that moment all she wanted was that they should have a decent funeral. She collected shrubs, twigs and dried leaves, and piled them on the three bodies. She begged neighbours for cow-dung cakes, which they used for cooking. Finally, she lit the three makeshift pyres she'd made, and desolately muttered a prayer.

Hundreds of Sikh women and children had gathered on the main roads, to weep, comfort and protect each other. Daljit Kaur preferred to stay alone and mourn by the pyres of her beloved family's men for the next two days and nights, as the madness around her continued unabated.

The mobs swelled in numbers and frenzy. That night, rumours spread that drinking water sources in the city had been poisoned by the Sikhs, and that trainloads of dead

Hindus, massacred by the Sikhs, had arrived at the Delhi railway station. Strangely, precisely these same rumours reverberated in cities and towns across the country.

A police jeep roamed the area, warning the Sikhs on loudspeakers that the police would not be responsible for their safety, and that they were on their own. Some Hindu neighbours sheltered Sikh families; a home of a Hindu family was burnt down in Trilokpuri because they had given refuge to their Sikh neighbours. Some Sikh men cropped their long hair, shaved off their beards and threw away their turbans to avoid being identified.

As the nightmarish nights and days unfolded, and Daljit Kaur kept vigil next to the now cold pyres, the air was heavy with the stench of rotting human flesh, mixed with burnt furniture and homes. Dogs and rats nibbled at the mass of half-burnt human bodies. Rampaging mobs passed her from time to time, but no one touched her.

Some of the Hindu men of the colony went to the Kalyanpuri station house officer, under whose jurisdiction Trilokpuri also falls, demanding protection for the surviving Sikhs in Trilokpuri. He refused to move, insisting that 'total peace' was reigning in the area.

In three days, at least 400 Sikh men were killed in Trilokpuri, which would later become infamous as the place of one of the worst mass killings in the aftermath of Indira Gandhi's death. Later, seven cases of rape from Trilokpuri were officially reported by the Jayaprakash Narayan Hospital in Delhi.

As Delhi burnt, the newly installed Home Minister P.V. Narasimha Rao, the Lt. Governor of Delhi, Wali, and the entire battery of magistrates and police officers, refused to take the help of the army to quell the riots. By contrast, the authorities had no difficulty in moving in a full brigade of the Indian army consisting of 3,000 men and another 1,000 personnel from the Navy and the Air Force to line the route of Indira Gandhi's funeral.

On the night of 2 November, the Central Reserve Police finally moved in to rescue the survivors in Trilokpuri. Daljit Kaur's turn came the next morning, and she asked to be taken to Anand Parbat. She did not know whether her mother-in-law and other brothers-in-law were still alive. She found to her relief that although they had been stoned, and their home and shop been burnt, they had survived the carnage. But it was left to her to break the terrible news to them.

Once again, Daljit's mother-in-law, Harnam Kaur, found herself in a relief camp. Once again she was left with nothing except the clothes that she wore. The difference was that this time she had lost also her husband and two grown sons. With her widowed daughter-in-law and surviving sons, Harnam Kaur once more made her long journey from the relief camp, to a gurudwara, and from there to a rented home, and then to a small tenement in a riot widows' colony in Tilak Vihar. She continues to share this place with her daughter-in-law, Daljit Kaur. Relief money eventually also came from the government—one hundred and ten thousand rupees for each person dead. It was described as 'compensation'. Most of the money was put in bank fixed deposits, and the interest helped keep the family together.

Sixteen years later, the eyes of both women still briefly well up as they recall the events of 1984. But Harnam Kaur and Daljit Kaur are hardy and strong women who have pushed their immense suffering behind them

resolutely, in order to help their families to carry on with
the business of living.

But below this surface calm, one thing rankles them
most of all—that after sixteen long years, hardly a single
person has been prosecuted for the carnage in Delhi, in
which more than 3,000 people were killed, and tens of
thousands rendered destitute. That after all that
happened, there has been no justice. Absolutely no justice.
And it is clear now that there will be no justice.

PAYING FOR HIS TEA

He is one among the few hundred people who sleep in and around Nizamuddin railway station in New Delhi each night. Amidst the medley of transit passengers who stretch out wherever they can on their bed-rolls, in the waiting room, or on the platform, are the regulars, mostly men and boys but also some women, who have made the railway station their home. There is no sign of them during the rush of travellers through the day. But once darkness falls, even though trains continue to come and go, the platforms and all the open spaces around the station silently fill up with people who have nowhere else to go. There are street children, beggars, street sex workers, people living with leprosy and mental illness, drug addicts, abandoned old people—a whole, separate world of people without a roof and anyone to take care of them, a microcosm of the invisible underbelly of the city. They have an uneasy relationship with the police and railway officials who on occasion evict them, sometimes brutally. They do not resist, but wait patiently for a few days, and then slowly, almost imperceptibly, they are back again. After all, they have no other home.

Amongst the regulars at Nizamuddin railway station, to be found there on most nights, is Shabir Singh, who lives by begging. He is a paraplegic, unable to move around on his feet. Instead, his strong arms bear his weight as he deftly drags himself around the place every day.

As we visited him at his permanent corner under a tree outside the station, he greeted us courteously. He wore nothing except striped blue underpants, his lifeless feet tucked below him, his head of hair full but grey, his age impossible to estimate. His belongings were squeezed into a small, faded cloth bag.

Gravely, he took out small sheets of cardboard from below where he sat, laid them out for us, and invited us to sit on them. As we talked, he insisted on calling for cups of tea from a nearby stall. It was as though he was entertaining us in his drawing room. Even though he had no home, begged for a living, could not walk without support, and wore few clothes, our overwhelming memory of him would be of his dignity.

During his childhood, neither his parents nor he could have dreamt of what fate held for him. The youngest of four brothers and one sister, Shabir's was a happy, carefree childhood. Their twelve bighas of canal-fed, fertile land in their village in Mainpuri district of Uttar Pradesh was more than enough to feed the large joint family. His two older brothers were recruited into the military. The army recruitment team came to the village itself to search for healthy young men who could be included in the ranks. It was assumed that Shabir would also join the army like his brothers.

He was fifteen when, in fraction of a second, his life changed forever. His brother had bought an orchard from the old village landlord. Shabir playfully climbed a tree, to cut firewood. In that fateful moment, his foot missed its step, he slipped and came crashing to the ground. His spine snapped, and he was crippled for life. He would never walk again.

His father had died a year earlier, but his mother with the help of people from the village, did all that they could to ensure that he got medical help. They even arranged for him to be taken to the large government hospital in Delhi, Safdarjang, where the doctor x-rayed his back, but even he was unable to give them hope. His mother continued to tend him, but she died some ten years later, broken by the truth of her son never being able to walk again.

Shabir was now completely in the hands of his brothers. His eldest brother, who had by then retired from the army and returned to the village, badgered him to give up his share of the agricultural land that they had inherited from their father. It is no use of you, he told him. You will never be able to cultivate it, and you will never have a family whom you will have to take care of. All that you need is some food and clothes, and a roof over your head. That I will always give you. Why don't you transfer your share in the ancestral property to me?

The villagers joined his brother in persuading him. He eventually relented, a decision he regrets to this day. His brother sold both their shares of the ancestral land, bought a house in the city, and shifted there, to turn his back forever on the village and the disabled Shabir. The brother who remained to take care of the fields, reluctantly fed Shabir, but all the while he made him feel he was an unwanted burden. Shabir decided eventually to move away, and not depend on anyone to take care of him in future.

There were many in his village who had trained to

become electricians and fitters, and had found work in
government departments in Delhi. They had observed
Shabir's predicament, and urged him to move to Delhi
with their help, and start a new life. They pooled some
money, and bought him an initial stock of agarbattis,
and a small trunk to store money and his belongings.
They took him to Delhi's main market, the colonial
Connaught Place, and found a place for him next to a
pillar in the circular corridor, in front of one of the
elegant shops.

It was there that he set up both shop and home for
some ten years. He earned enough to eat by selling the
incense sticks, and slept at night at the same spot, his iron
trunk firmly secured by a chain, bound to a shop's
shutters.

But Delhi had begun to change in these ten years.
Smack addicts and members of petty criminal gangs began
to threaten him and demand money. Finally, he decided to
close shop and return to his village. Maybe his brother
would have had a change of heart. Maybe he would accept
him more generously now.

He found his brother looking much older than when
he last saw him. But he had taken to drink and was even
more foul-mouthed than before. His brother's sons were
fond of him, and urged him to stay. But Shabir could not
bear the shame of being treated as a burden, and decided
to return again to the city of Delhi.

This time, there was no support. He tried once again
to ply his trade in Connaught Place, but unsuccessfully,
being too vulnerable to its harsh nocturnal underworld.
He decided instead to live now by begging. Over the years,
he has developed a routine. Outside the Tughlaqabad

railway station is the Peer Baba Mazaar, a small Muslim Sufi shrine. He sits outside it with his begging bowl. He has become a familiar sight for passers-by, who call him Baba. The Sikh owner of a small *dhaba* nearby got talking to him one day and learnt of his life story. Hearing it, he offered to feed him every night at his dhaba, and this arrangement has continued over the years.

Shabir catches the eleven o'clock night local train to return to Nizamuddin railway station, to his little corner of the pavement under the tree outside the station. There he settles down to sleep. In the morning, he drags himself to the neighbouring gurudwara, where he gets tea and breakfast. He takes the 3.20 p.m. train each afternoon to his 'work station' in Tughlaqabad station.

At Nizamuddin, he has been befriended by a tea-stall owner, young enough to be his grandson. When the boy saw the railway policemen occasionally harassing Shabir, he suggested that he should drag himself to next to the tea-stall whenever there was a police raid. He would tell the policemen that Shabir was his customer. The boy joined us when we were talking to Shabir. I have to pay the police people Rs 800 every month as bribe to run my tea-stall, he told us. They will not touch Baba, he said cockily, because they are in my pay and they know that he is my friend.

What impressed the young tea-stall owner most, initially, about Shabir was that although he was a disabled beggar, he insisted on always paying for his tea. It is one of Shabir's many rules that he will not beg in the area that he has made his home.

The years are passing for Shabir. Except for his brothers, he has no complaints against anyone. Yet an unspoken fear is that he will have to continue to beg until his dying day. My brother's son, my nephew, really loves me, he told us repeatedly. Maybe he will take care of me when my brother is no longer there, he adds wistfully. Maybe.

THE OBEISANCE

One summer morning in 1987, the district magistrate and the superintendent of police of Rajnandgaon in Chhatisgarh near Bhilai, received an urgent wireless message that a Satnami dalit had forcibly entered a Hindu temple, creating inter-caste tension that had escalated to become explosive.

The Satnami dalits in Chhatisgarh are both a religious sect and a caste. Under the influence of Guru Ghasidas, they formed a religious sect in the bhakti tradition, with their own religious symbols and priesthood. In practice, however, their forms of worship have been almost identical to those of other Hindus in the area. The Satnamis lay claim to a high social status, but all others place them at the bottom of the caste hierarchy, and they continue to experience severe discrimination, and even untouchability, in caste Hindu villages.

Barely two months earlier, there had been violence and bloodshed in a village bordering the district of Rajnandgaon, in Bilaspur, after a procession of Satnamis attempted to force their way into a Hindu temple. Therefore, when the DM and SP received fresh news of the forcible temple entry by a Satnami in a border village of their district, it is not surprising that they rushed to the village, driving their jeep through the district's dusty and narrow roads at breakneck speed.

At the village police station, the DM and SP expected to meet a hardened criminal. The man they encountered there turned out to be completely the opposite. He was young, obviously very poor, and absolutely terrified. He fell at their feet, crying, I have made a great mistake, but I meant no harm. Please forgive me. I have committed a grave wrong, but I did it unknowingly. The officers were rather bewildered at the man's apology, and were not certain if they should believe him. It needed a lot of coaxing to make the man speak. But, bit by bit, his story emerged.

Mohan was an impoverished landless labourer, who had no one he could call his own except for his wife whom he loved dearly. Once she fell so seriously ill that he began to despair about her ever recovering. He then made a vow, that if she recovered, he would make a special offering to Hanuman called 'chola chadao', or literally, to dress Lord Hanuman in a tunic. A paste of *sindoor* and pure ghee was to be applied, in accordance with the local ritual, on an image of the deity.

Mohan's wife recovered eventually, and he set about honouring his vow. With great difficulty he saved enough money and bought what was required for the ritual. Then Mohan proceded to the shrine of Hanuman. It was little more than an idol placed under peepul tree, not a grand temple in honour of the deity. Mohan had just begun reverentially to apply his paste of sindoor and ghee to the idol, when an upper-caste boy spotted him. Then all hell broke loose.

The boy quickly gathered his friends, who shared his outrage at their village deity being polluted by an untouchable. Together they thrashed Mohan. Fortunately, the police station was located in the same village and the police arrived barely in time to rescue Mohan.

Meanwhile, the tension in the village was palpable, the mood in the upper-caste segment of the village was one of sullen outrage. The boys were cowed by the massive display of khaki, as extra forces were rushed into the village and pickets appeared at sensitive points. For their part, the Satnamis of the village were sullen and angry, but too frightened and unorganized to openly come out in defence of Mohan. Privately, upper-caste Hindus insisted on revenge for what they saw as Mohan's unforgivable act of sacrilege. The Satnamis were forgetting their station; the boys declared that they would not rest until they settled scores. They resolved to do this by urinating not only on Mohan's head, but also on the most sacred Satnami religious symbol. The latter was a log of wood, planted upright in the Satnami quarter; it was the object of much of the local worship. Only by thus desecrating the Satnami's symbol, and punishing Mohan did the upper-caste boys feel they could avenge the sacrilege that had been committed by Mohan.

The DM called a meeting in the village and tried to reason with the caste-Hindu boys and their elders. He argued: How can you equate what Mohan did, in showing the utmost devotion possible to your gods, with what the boys are planning to do to, namely, desecrating the Satnami sacred symbol? But no one was willing to listen to reason. The DM and SP then came down with a heavy hand, arresting many of the upper-caste boys. Mohan was now too frightened to continue to live in the village; he soon left the place with his wife, under police protection, for another district, to live with a distant relative.

Police pickets continued in the small remote village for forty days, before they could be withdrawn. But it was several months before Mohan felt he could return to the village of his birth and pick up the threads of his humble life once again.

THE LAMINATED MARKSHEET

A young boy Satyakam went to Gautam rishi because
he wished to learn the Vedas from him. Before
accepting him as his student, the rishi asked the boy
his caste.
The boy replied, without flinching, 'My mother was a
prostitute who lived in this ashram and would service
the visitors here. I, therefore, have no way of knowing
my caste.'
Greatly impressed by the boy's courage and honesty,
the rishi declared that the boy was truly of the highest
caste, not by virtue of his birth, but by his actions,
and he gladly admitted him into his ashram.

—A story from the *Chandogya Upanishad* (cu. iv. 4)

We had barely settled in our chairs in Geeta's modest but
neat home in the small district town of Shivpuri, when she
held out some laminated papers to us. It was clear that
they were her most valued possessions. When we looked
at the papers, we found them to be her elder son's
marksheet for the class twelve examination. She proudly
pointed out to us his aggregate percentage, of 83 per cent.

Geeta, ravaged by her long years of sex work, and her
agonizing struggle to move beyond it, looks much older
than her thirty-three years. Her husband, Rajendra, is not
much older than her elder son. Together they have fought,

quietly and courageously, a battle against those beliefs and practices of their own community which they regard as intolerably inhuman and unjust. But, in so doing they have also disregarded some of the taboos of the mainstream. They now find themselves isolated, sometimes to the point of despair. At such times, it is the precious laminated marksheet, and their sons' caring support, that revives their spirits.

Geeta and Rajendra belong to the Bedia community, in which a little-known form of ritually-sanctioned caste-based sex work is practised even today. In the shadow of the feudal, rural society of Madhya Pradesh and Rajasthan, masses of young Bedia girls are drawn into the profession of sex work only because of the accident of their birth into this caste. In a system that is supported by a complex alternative matrix of social mores, the daughter of the family is introduced into sex work by her own mother and male members of her family. The women engaged in this profession are brought up to be the bread-winners of the family, whereas the male members do little more than solicit clients for their daughters, sisters or mothers, or engage in petty crime, or simply remain idle.

The principal castes in Madhya Pradesh in which such ritually-sanctioned caste-based sex work is widely prevalent are the Bancharas and Bedias. In addition, there are other denotified tribes such as the Nat, Sansi and Kanjar, in which tradition and caste mores sanction and support the pursuit of petty criminal activity. In these castes, it is considered a matter of masculine pride not to purchase or grow the food which they consume, but instead to steal or snatch it. However, ritual and caste traditions and mores do not support sex work as among the Bancharas and Bedias.

There is no authentic recorded history of the evolution of caste-based sex work among the Bancharas and Bedias. However, there is evidence to suggest it is of relatively recent origin and that the traditional occupation of Bedias in ancient, and even medieval times was not sex work. A complex series of historical circumstances led to them taking to caste-based sex work.

The princely states of India, prior to the consolidation of British rule in India, were frequently at war with one another. The large mobile armies raised by the warring princely states required major auxillary services of reconnaissance, espionage and entertainment. For this, the nomadic tribes like Bancharas and Bedias were best equipped. These tribes were traditionally skilled in folk music and dance, rural acrobatics and gymnastics, jugglery, fortune telling and black magic. These skills made them ideal auxillaries to armies on the move. They also engaged to some extent in sex work, but this did not have ritual and social sanction, and was carried on covertly.

When the British arrived in India at the close of the seventeenth century, the power of the princely states began to break down. After the First War of Indian Independence of 1857 was quelled, there was a full imposition of pax Brittanica. Wars between princely states almost passed into history. The new military arrangements of the states were based on the principles of defence and displays of grandeur rather than aggression, and their control had passed effectively into the hands of the British. The military no longer needed the services of the nomadic tribes, and the patronage and protection of the princely states also collapsed.

In these changed circumstances, the nomadic tribes, including the Banacharas and Bedias, took to organized loot and dacoity as their principal means of livelihood. They came to be greatly feared, and commerce and trade which was conducted largely through caravans of camels, bullock-carts and mules, was seriously hampered by the terror spread by these tribes.

The British administration classified them as criminal tribes, and their activities were closely monitored by the police. For their own protection, these communities carried on being on the move, and eked out a livelihood by petty crime, fashioning utensils and other domestic items, selling medicinal herbs, taming wild animals for use in village entertainment shows, acrobatics, gymnastics and jugglery.

Those groups that possessed some technical skill gradually got absorbed into the rural society as artisans. However, those who were engaged in providing services, such as the entertainers, were unable to secure a stable, alternative source of livelihood. Because in the campaign against thuggi they were identified as criminal tribes, the police would round them up, with or without justification, whenever any crime occurred. This not only reinforced their nomadic character, but also resulted in males spending large periods either in jails or as fugitives from the law, away from their families.

The burden of protecting and supporting their families fell directly on the women. As they lacked any skills except that of the increasingly outdated village entertainment, they were often forced to sell their bodies in order to sustain their families. Initially, the men resisted the entry of their women into this profession. But given their circumstances, they were obliged to compromise despite their aggrieved masculine pride. In time, the community, defensively invoked the social mechanisms of ritual and tradition to transform sex work into a socially acceptable source of family and group livelihood.

The Bedia women are traditionally skilled in folk dances with sexual overtones. They are frequently taken as mistresses by the rural rich, in which case they remain monogamous and loyal to their keepers. Other women engage in sex work with several men. The initiation of a daughter into sex work is an occasion for celebration, on the scale of a wedding.

The Bedias came to be listed in the Indian constitution as scheduled castes. Based on projections from the 1981 census data, it is estimated that in Madhya Pradesh there are a total of 16,682 Bedias, or approximately 3,124 families. 88.57 per cent of the Bedias reside in the rural areas. The social and ritual sanction accorded to this profession and the severe social ostracism faced by the Bedias in society at large, together with the absence of alternative sources of employment, are responsible for most Bedia families engaging in sex work. Some of them, however, are struggling to relieve themselves from its grip.

It is not possible to generalize about the economic status of the Bedias. They span much of the economic spectrum, ranging on the one hand from those engaged in urban sex work, with high incomes and a visible upper middle-class consumerist lifestyle, to the very poor landless, highway rural prostitutes. There are several instances of women being purchased for red-light areas in the metropolises, or as mistresses. The infamous case of Kamala, a Bedia girl of Morena, who was purchased by a correspondent of the *Indian Express*, initially raised a storm but has been subsequently all but forgotten. Recently, some groups of Bedia women have even travelled abroad for sex work as part of so-called cultural troupes, especially to the Gulf countries, and have returned with very substantial incomes. We have seen Bedia families in Morena, for instance, who used very expensive consumer durables like the best Indian cars, VCRs, refrigerators and the like. The women who are taken as mistresses by the rural rich enjoy greater economic security, but this practice is becoming much more rare and is increasingly being replaced by casual sex work. At the other extreme, there are rural settlements of such traditional caste-based sex workers who live in very sparse hutments, with very few household goods, little economic security and hardly enough income to sustain their families.

The social status of the women within the family is complex. There is no doubt that because the woman is the bread-winner, she enjoys a degree of independence and control within her family and social set-up that is not found in other caste groups. There being no taboo against sex work, the social status of women practising it is often higher than that of married women.

This enhanced socio-economic status of the women is reflected in the sex ratio being in favour of women in the community (54 per cent among the Bedias), in sharp contrast to the adverse sex ratio prevalent in general in the

Indian subcontinent, and even more so in the feudal stranglehold of the Gwalior region. This probably reflects better nutrition and health care of females, in contrast to their neglect in other communities.

However, literacy levels are abysmally low, even more so among the women. Literacy among Bedia women is 7.8 per cent, which is much lower than the Bedia men at 27.25 per cent. The men of the community at present are largely engaged either in petty crime, especially stealing grain and cattle, and soliciting clients for the women of the family. However, as compared to men of other communities, they have less control over both decision-making and property within the family.

As we have seen, the caste-based sex work of the Bedia community is largely rural, but in a few exceptional pockets like the small district town of Shivpuri where Geeta and Rajendra live, its urban variation is not unlike that of the conventional, red-light areas. Some of the Bedia girls sold to brothels in metropolises have even been known to travel to Arab countries.

Into such a home in Gwalior, Rajendra was born twenty-five years ago to a Bedia mother. When he was a child, she plied her trade mostly from home, and he did not understand what she did to bring home enough money to feed his three elder sisters, a younger brother and himself. When he was a little older, they shifted to the small settlement of Bedias in the district town of Shivpuri. Bedia families from villages in the region had over the past decade migrated there in search of better prospects in the profession, and gradually this settlement of around seventy Bedia homes came up at the edge of the city.

As his sisters, one by one, took to sex work, and many strange men came to spend the nights in their home with his mother and sisters, it was not long before the young boy understood fully for the first time what it means to be born a Bedia.

The trauma he experienced was greatest when his mother admitted him to the local, government primary school. She crossed out the column in his school entry form requiring his father's name, and instead entered her own. He soon learnt that his father's name being unacknowledged had revealed to the world his mother's profession. His classmates shunned his company, and often openly taunted him. His teachers made no effort to disguise their disapproval and revulsion. Rajendra recalls with reverence only one teacher, Gopal Garg, who encouraged the Bedia children, and never made them feel that they were lesser people. When Rajendra entered secondary school, his mother took care not to cancel the column requiring his father's name; she put in a fictitious name, and added 'late' before it.

However, in a small town like Shivpuri, it was impossible for Rajendra to hide his identity. There were many times when he felt humiliated and anguished, and would fight with his mother. On such occasions, she would caress and comfort him, pleading softly, What other way was there for me to bring up all of you? I know who your father is, a rich jeweller in Gwalior. But he will never acknowledge you. I was brought up like every Bedia woman, deeply conscious of my responsibility to earn for and take care of my brothers and sons. If we do not take up this work, what will become of the men in our families?

Who will take care of them? I know my work causes you shame. But I know no other way to take care of you.

Rajendra slowly came to understand the huge gap between the ethical norms of his community and the world beyond it. Traditionally, all Bedia girls were debarred from marriage, and it was mandatory that they take up the profession of sex work. Any contravention of this rule would lead to the expulsion of the family from the community. Men wanting to marry had to seek out girls of other communities with which the Bedias had affinity, like the Nats and Kanjars, or girls who were orphaned and abandoned.

Today, a Bedia girl can choose to do sex work or to marry, but this freedom is nominal. In practice, she is still influenced by her socialization and her conviction that it is primarily, almost exclusively, her responsibility to support her family through sex work. If a Bedia girl marries, there are strong taboos against her engaging in sex work. But a woman who chooses to marry is perceived to be selfish, callous and negligent. Not surprisingly, even today, less than half of Bedia women (44 per cent accordingly to the 1981 census) marry, the rest, following custom, take to sex work in their teens to support their families. A girl's initiation into sex work is a major occasion for celebration among the Bedias, very similar to a wedding. And as women grow older, and the attention they receive from clients declines, they are desperate for girl children to introduce into sex work. Rajendra's mother was no different, and she initiated all three of his sisters into her profession.

As a result, for Bedia men brides are hard to find; the 1981 census reveals that over 53 per cent of Bedia men are unmarried. Men have to pay an exhorbitant bride-price to secure brides, and to compensate the bride's family for the loss of an earning member. Women slave in sex work most of all to collect the bride-price for their sons and brothers. The same dream motivated Rajendra's mother and sisters.

Despite such a shortage of brides, the strongest taboo amongst the Bedia men is to marry a girl who is a sex worker. Therefore, when Rajendra took to spending long hours with Geeta, a sex worker several years older to him, and distantly related, the disapproval was vociferous. They both insisted that their relationship was platonic, but many did not believe them.

Rajendra was initially drawn to Geeta, most of all because despite herself being mired in the shadowy world of sex work, she still aspired, secretly and fervently, for a better life for her two sons. She would never tire of telling them that it was only by educating themselves they could break free from the vicious cycle that was their fate. Her elder son, born when she was thirteen, was not much younger than Rajendra. Slightly disabled, he developed an obsession for books like her, and it was only Rajendra whom they called 'elder brother' who could draw him away for a few minutes of play.

Rajendra was a college student of eighteen, when he went with half a dozen Bedia friends to a meeting of the community in neighbouring Morena. The meeting, the first of its kind in the history of the Bedia community, was organized by some administrators, and officials of the state government's department of scheduled castes and scheduled tribes. They sought to facilitate processes of change within the community, together with an elderly reformer from the community, Ram Sanehi. Ram Sanehi had fought many lonely battles against practices of his community which preyed on young girls. Years of persecution and ostracism by the mainstream of his community had not restrained or dampened his fervour.

Rajendra was enormously excited by what he heard in the meeting, about the inhumanity and injustice of a system of which he had been a part since his childhood. One Bedia girl, barely in her teens, stood up and bravely declared, it is not caste but a person's actions and character that determine his or her future, and I am going to prove this to the world.

In the voices of the young of his community, Rajendra heard, for the first time, the breaking of chains.

Along with some friends, Rajendra organized at Shivpuri the first-ever gathering of Bedia families, aimed at group introspection. In the meeting, which was also attended by town folk outside the community, he stood up and declared openly like Satyakam centuries before him, I am the illegitimate child of a Seth who will never acknowledge me. My mother, and now my sisters have brought me up through sex work. This must end. And we must end it by working together.

Following this meeting, Rajendra resolved never to marry, and to break out of the vicious cycle faced by Bedia men, as they depended on their mothers and sisters to earn a bride-price for them, and which pressed them into sex work. But his growing closeness to Geeta and her boys, and the push of some local activists, spurred him to take a decision that he realized would be a much more powerful indictment of the Bedia system. He declared that he would marry Geeta.

Both their families were devastated. The taboo against

a Bedia man marrying a sex worker of his community was so powerful that the couple was sure to be expelled forever from the Bedia community. To make matters worse, Geeta was much older to him, and her sons were almost Rajendra's age. However, the worst blow fell when Geeta revealed to them that she had had herself sterilized after the birth of her two sons. She had resolved at that time that she wanted no daughters, which in her community was very unusual, as it was daughters who were most valued. But Geeta had quietly determined that she did not want a daughter as she would be drawn inexorably into sex work. This cycle of shame and pain, given in legacy from women of one generation to the next, must end in her family with her.

This now meant that Rajendra would never have children of his own. His mother and sisters reasoned with him, that it was bad enough he would be expelled from his community, but how could he allow the family line also to end with him. Rajendra said that he would regard Geeta's sons as his own. But, they argued, Geeta's sons were almost his own age, and they would never regard him as a father. Despite these objections, Rajendra was steadfast in his decision.

Geeta's mother, on her part, was most of all terrified about her own future when Geeta's earnings stopped pouring in.

Rejected so completely by their community and families, Geeta and Rajendra moved into a tiny tenement after their marriage, to start their new life together. He took a loan to run an auto-rickshaw, which he plies to date. Even today they survive on the earnings from it; these are uncertain and insufficient, as the small town has far more rickshaws than it can support. The local government officials had promised to assist the couple with grants of land and jobs, but nothing has so far come their way. Geeta adjusted quickly to the role of a housekeeper, and pursued her sons' studies with redoubled fervour. A saving grace was that she did not have to fill a fictitious father's name in the school admission form. Her children now had a legal father.

Throughout the five years of marriage, their social ostracism has continued. The mainstream of the Bedia caste is unrelenting, and regards the couple as dangerous troublemakers, who might mislead women who are today dutifully supporting their families with sex work. Their own families, however, have slowly accepted them, reluctantly influenced by their resolute courage and steadfastness. Geeta's mother has even allowed them to live in her home.

However, the small town refuses to forget their past. To date, it is impossible for the two to walk the streets without searing taunts and jeers following them. Old customers still bang at their door at night; and some months back a drunken group even broke down their door. They still do not have the money to repair it.

Money is always short, and it is years since the couple remembers buying new clothes for themselves, or living comfortably. Outside their home, in the same neighbourhood, Bedia families prosper on the earnings of their women, and it is Geeta and Rajendra's family that stands apart for what is regarded as their stubborn foolhardiness.

But, in their household, there are no regrets. Rajendra remains 'elder brother' to the boys in the privacy of their homes, although they call him Papa for public consumption. The boys greatly respect and value both their parents, for the courage and sacrifice of their decisions, and they study hard, almost obsessively. It is this, and this alone, that will get you respect, their mother intones almost daily. Study, study, study, and earn the respect which no one can challenge.

In the bleak desolation of rejection, the couple cherishes rare instances of acceptance and respect. They remember the doctor who has notified the local chemist that Geeta is like a daughter to him, and, therefore, any expenses on medicine for her family should be billed to him. Or the senior and respected lawyer of the town who came himself to their home, with an invitation for his daughter's wedding. Imagine—they told me with great pride—the wedding card itself was worth Rs 25. And the lawyer said to the couple, There can be no greater privilege for me, than that a courageous couple like you comes to the wedding to bless my daughter.

But in the end it is the laminated marksheet of their elder son, with his proud achievement of 83 per cent, rarely matched in a small town, and the loving ways of the children, that makes it all seem worthwhile in the end. The last eight months they have struggled and saved so that the elder boy could attend a coaching institute in Gwalior, to prepare him for the entrance exa.nination for medical college. They dream of the day when he will be able to hold his head high as a doctor. That day, their life will be fulfilled.

Postscript: After I had completed this story, I received a telephone call before dawn, when concessional rates apply to long-distance calls. The callers were Rajendra and Geeta. Their voices on the phone line were faint, but I could still hear the bursting pride.

Their son had secured admission in medical college.

TOGETHER AS ONE PEOPLE

The storm-clouds gathered over the country with terrifying speed. It was the autumn of 1989. In the short space of a few unendurably tension-racked weeks, the country changed course so fundamentally that the many values and beliefs which held us together as one people seemed to be relentlessly and inexorably swept aside. The Bharatiya Janata Party, and its assemblage of front organizations espousing a militant Hindutva ideology announced the launching of direct action to build a Ram temple at the disputed site of the Babri masjid at Ayodhya. The legal and political processes to achieve this agenda were pushed on to the back-burner; now there would be an open, and if necessary, bloody battle of confrontation.

This new mood of belligerence manifested itself in the countrywide Ram Shila Poojan programme which was launched on 15 September 1989. In the space of the next few days, the country was seized by a frenzy unprecedented since Partition. Groups of surcharged young men paraded the streets in every town, morning and evening, day after day, aggressively bearing bricks with the name of Ram for the construction of a Ram temple at the site of the doomed Babri masjid. They hurled slogans, like acid, which were astounding in their virulence, crudeness and naked aggression at the Muslims. The Muslims, huddled in their ghettoes, watched with disbelief and horror, and which rapidly turned into cold terror and sullen anger. For many, the faith and hope built doggedly over four decades soured. Avowedly secular governments across the country, except West Bengal, refused to ban the explosive Ram Shila Poojan programme, the media and intelligentsia were quickly infected by the communal dementia sweeping the land, and even secular voices corroborated through their deafening silence.

In less than ten days, town after town, in a grim roll-call, succumbed to blood-drenched rioting and curfew. The sequence was repeated with aching uniformity—militant processions brandishing bricks stamped with Ram, and shouting hate-filled slogans, violent retaliation by small Muslim groups, followed by the madness of carnage, deaths, arson, and finally curfew. At one point, around three weeks after the programme was launched, as many as 108 towns were simultaneously under curfew.

It was futile to expect the small district town of Khargone in western Madhya Pradesh to remain untouched by the sectarian fever that had seized the land. An undersized, haphazardly planned town of less than one lakh persons, with an uneasy balance between its equal number of Hindus and Muslims, Khargone was classified in official files as being highly sensitive communally. The records show that the first communal clash took place as far back as 1921, when Khargone was the capital of a tiny and modest principality, and these clashes were repeated with frightening regularity over the following decades. The

issues were mostly local, such as attacks on religious
processions, desecration of shrines, and relationships
between men and women of different communities. The
two communities lived cheek by jowl in crowded, sunless
shanties, and any small spark could set off a bloody
confrontation. Each clash would leave behind its own
fresh trail of hostility and suspicion.

With such an accumulated history of hatred and
prejudice between the two communities, it was only a
matter of time before the conflagration sweeping the
country also seared the town of Khargone. The town's
young DM and SP responded by calling meetings of the
two communities, and advised restraint, registration of
strong criminal charges against the processionists,
energizing of peace committees, and preventive arrests.
However, these measures, adequate perhaps in normal
times, could not ebb the raging flood of communal hatred.

The flashpoint was rapidly reached in less than a
fortnight, when the district-wide Ram Shila Poojan
programme was to climax in a massive procession in
Khargone on 30 September 1989. Late that night, Bajrang
Dal and Vishwa Hindu Parishad volunteers were busy
transforming the town into a saffron stronghold, with a
profusion of flags, posters, slogans and buntings.
Suddenly out of the darkness, two Muslim youths, their
faces masked by burqas, appeared on a motorcycle,
flashing daggers, and stabbed two young men who were
painting slogans. In the government hospital, night-long,
emergency operations saved the lives of the two victims,
but tension in the town was acutely palpable.

Several arrests were made through the night, and at
dawn, leaders of the various Hindutva organizations were

summoned to the police station for an emergency meeting
with the DM and SP. The appeals of the district officers
for a cancellation or postponement of the Ram Shila
Poojan programme that morning were stubbornly
rejected, as also any suggestions for changing the route so
as to altogether avoid Muslim settlements and mosques.
Already some twenty-five to thirty thousand Hindutva
volunteers had assembled, determined and greatly
charged. The DM and SP realized that any attempt to halt
the procession by force at this stage was doomed to
failure, and would lead only to widescale violence and
killings. The only option seemed to be to let the procession
pass, but with intensive control and regulation.

The procession was unprecedented in size, passion
and militancy. All assurances given earlier in writing by
the organizers regarding restraint in sloganeering were
thrown to the winds, and the most vulgar and vicious
slogans rent the air. Trishuls and naked daggers were
flashed. The leaders suddenly attempted to steer the
procession into the heart of the Muslim bastis, again in
violation of the prior agreement, but they were firmly
pushed back on to the agreed route.

The seemingly endless procession wound its way
slowly and tortuously through the narrow lanes, as
tension mounted to an unbearable level. In particular, as
the procession passed the mosques, the virulence and the
passion of the sloganeering reached a new pitch, and the
magistrates and police took care to physically push the
frenzied young men forward and keep the procession
moving. No Muslim was to be seen out of doors.

About two-thirds of the procession had passed by late
afternoon, and the DM and SP were somewhat relieved

and thought that the explosive situation had been defused, at least for that day. They were standing at the crossroads before one particular mosque, which had been the site of several communal clashes in the past, and where the frenzy of any Hindu procession would traditionally reach its climax. The DM and SP kept pushing forward the crowd, acutely alert in case there should be a clash.

Suddenly, a bunch of panic-stricken young men came running in the opposite direction to meet the procession. They shouted that the Muslims had thrown a bomb on the crowd and a processionist has been killed. The DM and SP ran to the spot, barely hundred metres away. There they encountered a young man, his chest torn open by a crude bomb, his life quickly ebbing away. The DM quickly lifted the boy into his car which was parked nearly, and asked the driver to rush him to hospital. Before the car could reach the hospital the boy died.

The story of the bomb attack unfolded during later investigations. The daily and repeated battery of vitriolic sloganeering by mobs of youth entering Muslim bastis had terrorized the community. A small group of eight youth, two of them petty government servants—a forest guard and a patwari—then decided that they must retaliate. And because they felt alienated, both from the police system and their own community, which they felt was too passive, they decided to resort to a secret terrorist-type attack.

Collecting a few hundred rupees between them, they used the money to clandestinely purchase gunpowder from a cottage unit manufacturing firecrackers in the neighbouring district of Dhar. The night before the major Ram Shila procession, they stayed up in an abandoned ruin by the riverside. They ground the gunpowder with pieces of broken glass and old rusted nails, tied these in newspaper with a string, to make seventeen of what are known in local parlance as 'soothli bombs'.

Their game plan became clear to the DM and SP as soon as they reached the spot after the first bomb was thrown. The bomb was hurled on the mob from a small double-storeyed house in a very narrow by-lane, which branched off from the main lane through which the procession was passing. The calculation clearly was that the enraged mob would gather below the house to attack it and set it on fire, and a series of bombs would be thrown from above on the mob, resulting in a large number deaths.

The DM and SP quickly assessed the situation, and realized that the only way the mob could be prevented from assembling below the house from which the bomb was thrown, was if they themselves went there and took charge of the situation. The risk of their being hurt by the bombs was great, but acceptable if a far bigger tragedy could be prevented.

The DM and SP repeatedly shouted to the mob that they should stay away, and that they were taking charge of the situation. Most of the crowd listened and, tentatively, kept off. Once below the house, the best course appeared to be to fire at the house from which the bomb was thrown. The SP himself, and ASI who accompanied him, fired a repeated volley of rounds at the house. This served several purposes. The crowd was satisfied that effective action was being taken, and did not insist on taking the law into their own hands. The continuous volley of bullets also ensured that the crowd did not venture below the house, thereby averting further bomb-casualties. The firing also frightened the conspirators and stopped them from throwing any more bombs. While running away from the rear of the house, one of them was caught by the police, and it was through him that the police case was subsequently solved.

The crowd now began to fan out in every direction, and many rushed straight into the Muslim bastis. The DM immediately ordered curfew, and went on to the mobile wireless to instruct the police and magistrates already on duty in pickets at all sensitive points in the town, to impose curfew with a firm hand in the shortest possible time, using whatever force necessary including resort to firing. The DM and SP jumped into the SP's jeep, and they drove to the sensitive bastis. The SP himself fired several rounds. The police resorted to firing at three other places. Curfew was fully imposed in the brief space of twenty minutes.

However, even in these twenty minutes, four lives were lost and about a hundred Muslim houses and commercial establishments set ablaze, and three mosques desecrated. The deaths were an outcome of the country-made rifles and daggers, used by the mobs assaulting the Muslim bustees, and a bomb thrown by the fleeing group.

At one point, the SP spotted a frenzied young man brandishing a .12 bore rifle. The SP jumped off his jeep and walked towards the young man, who threatened to shoot at him. Undeterred, the SP slowly moved towards the young man, overpowered him, snatched his rifle, and forced him into a nearby house which he locked from the outside.

Soon an uneasy calm fell over the city. Forces were called in from neighbouring districts, and permanent pickets established at all sensitive points. All magistrates were pressed into duty, and police patrolling was now intensified throughout the city night and day. Large-scale preventive arrests and searches were ordered. The first night itself 126 persons were arrested, but most of them were Muslim. Forty houses were searched. The families of the deceased were contacted, and quiet cremations and burials organized in the presence only of close family members, the magistrates and the police. The injured were rushed to hospitals.

There was no relaxation of curfew for seventy-two hours, and little violation of it, except notably that four more mosques were extensively desecrated on the second night. The anguished Muslim community insisted that this could not have been possible without police complicity.

The DM and SP snatched two hours of sleep the second night in the police station. They would spend the next nineteen nights here, at first on benches under a tree, and later on camp-cots in a tent, fully dressed and ready to rush at the report of any clash. For the rest of the time, they were constantly on patrol. The people of Khargone were to become familiar with their white Gypsy and its flashing red light, endlessly scouring the shadowy and deserted lanes and by-lanes of the city. The control room was assailed by a continuous barrage of complaints of mob assault, all of which were checked out, and most proved to be rumours. The press was called and briefed, and arrangements made for the distribution of newspapers from the second day, in order to control rumours. The peace committee and responsible leaders of the two communities were pressed into service to restore normalcy.

From the morning after the incident, senior officials and ministers descended on the town, culminating in the visit by helicopter of the chief minister the second afternoon. They met senior citizens and victims, expressed grief at the killings, and by and large endorsed the action of the district administration. The relief at the visit of the chief minister going off peacefully, was so great, that as the DM and SP sat squashed together in the front seat of the CM's car when they drove him to the helipad, the DM quietly reached out for the hand of the SP and pressed it. His colleague reciprocated likewise.

Following this, the deluge of VIPs reduced, because large parts of the state were simultaneously racked by similar and more virulent communal violence. Only the district minister stayed on. She told the DM that she was there only to extend support, and would act just as he desired. He asked her to address the peace committee the next morning, and then visit the bereaved families, and the injured in hospital, as also the desecrated mosques. Her genuine anguish and sympathy did a little to assuage the raw wounds of the victims.

The DM mobilized the services of the Public Works' Department to repair and restore overnight the desecrated mosques, with the support of moderate Muslim leaders, before the first relaxation of curfew, for two hours. The Muslims wended their way straight to the mosques to offer prayers, but the fresh paint and mortar told their own story, and they responded in low voices and with sombre ashen faces. The settlements which had suffered arson looked as if they had been bombed. But except for an explosion in which no one was injured just before curfew relaxation was to end, there were no major setback when curfew was eased for the first time.

In the days and nights that unfolded, in the uneasy, taut, silence of a town under curfew, the jeep of the DM and SP endlessly wound through the narrow, eerie and deserted lanes and by-ways, to maintain—or impose—a most fragile peace. Among the crowded images of that time, there were some that would remain impressed on their hearts and minds for a lifetime.

On the second morning of curfew, a message was flashed on the mobile wireless that over two hundred women and children in a Muslim *mohalla* had poured on to the streets, in stubborn defiance of the curfew. The DM and SP rushed there, and amidst the disconsolate weeping of children, the women complained, There is now not a grain of food or a drop of milk in our homes. Our men have either been rounded up by the police or have run away and are in hiding. We earn from day-to-day and eat. How long can we let our children starve?

The DM at the police station immediately sent for all senior district officers, and gave them the charge of ensuring civil supplies in designated colonies of the town. The wholesale traders were asked to open their godowns, and district officers organized mobile vans with essential commodities for each mohalla. Curfew was lifted only for women during the visits of the mobile vans to each mohalla, during which time they made their purchases. For the poorest dalit bastis, the

DM ordered that ten kilograms of grain be distributed free to each family, because being so poor they had no savings whatsoever to purchase the grain. He promised the traders that the district administration would make good the cost by donations later.

The police force in those days was stretched almost unendurably. Since the Ram Shila Poojan programme had commenced a fortnight earlier the armed constabulary had been on continuous vigil in neighbouring districts. The riot at Khargone ensured that they were hastily bundled on to buses and trucks and overnight driven to the town, where they were immediately deputed to man every sensitive spot.

The DM and SP made it a point during their own night-long rounds to stop at each of the pickets, speak to the men about how difficult but how important was their mission, and occasionally share a hot cup of tea with them. The two officers would often recall with warmth later on how the weary faces of the men would light up with just this interchange. Before the men left weeks later for the next riot-torn city, the DM persuaded the eminent citizens of the town to organize a thanksgiving bada khana for the men, in which they sat and ate as the city elders served them.

Four days after the bomb attack, the DM from neighbouring Indore telephoned to say that one of the seriously injured riot victims from Khargone, a young man Ghulam, had died in the medical college in Indore, and that the district officers of Khargone should arrange for the disposal of the body. Communal tension had risen also in Indore, and they could not risk organizing the funeral there.

The DM and SP sent for the young man's father, and the *sadar* or city leader of the Muslim community, a humane and gentle Rauf Bhai, and they both agreed to a quiet funeral after midnight so as to prevent a fresh upsurge of violence. The morgue van carrying the body from Indore was halted at a rural thana at the outskirts of the town, to await the midnight hour.

The DM and SP decided to go thana to offer solace to the bereaved family. They encountered the mother weeping desolately near the body of her son, and the father and the sadar grieving nearby. The DM quietly said, We cannot bring back your son. But tell us who was responsible for your loss and we will ensure that justice is done.

The mother replied angrily, There is no point telling you the names of the killers. Every time in Khargone when there are riots, the same men lead the mobs, looting, burning and killing, but nothing ever happens to them. The last riots, we were hopeful because the police even noted our statements. We waited for four days, but nothing happened. In the end the police did come, but it was we who were arrested. Therefore, we have nothing to say.

The DM promised them that this time justice would be done, and pressed them for the names. They finally gave the names—among then were some of the most powerful and prestigious men of the district. The DM said to the SP, let us round them all up before the body of this boy is lowered into the dust.

It was after midnight that the body was driven to the graveyard, a brush-covered wilderness outside the town, and carried in the cold, moonless darkness to the burial spot. Before the grave was dug, and the body lowered into it, the jeep of the SP arrived, and the SP flashing his torchlight rushed to the DM who was with the bereaved family, and said, Sir, they have all been arrested.

It was around three o'clock in the morning when the DM and SP got back to their tent in the police station, and wearily stretched out, fully dressed, to catch a little sleep. Two hours later, at dawn, they were awakened by an uproar at the thana gates. Sleepily rubbing their eyes, they found that the local MLA of the ruling party had arrived with a group of her supporters, all holding curfew passes.

Injustice, injustice, she was crying out with her supporters. We will not put up with this injustice. We will not allow the arrest of innocent people.

The DM quickly understood what had happened, and was furious. Tell me, he asked her, are you the representative of one community or of this town? The last few days, when hundreds of Muslims were arrested, beaten, dragged by their beards, and placed behind bars, with no criminal records, no complaint against them, I never heard even a whimper of protest from you. But last night, because ten Hindu men have been arrested, after complaints of murder, you march here within two hours and shout of injustice.

He directed her to leave the thana premises immediately and refused to discuss the issue any further.

The MLA's march was only the beginning. The whole day witnessed more pressure than the DM had experienced in a single day on any issue during his frequently turbulent career. The chief minister telephoned to enquire about the outrage. The DM replied that it was a matter of basic justice, and he would not change his decision. He was relieved that the CM did not get back to him. But from the state capital downwards, the pressure continued to mount. The DM advised the district minister to quietly leave because she was finding the dispute unbearable.

Late that night, according to their daily routine since the tension had broken out, the DM and SP sat at the thana reviewing the arrests and releases of the day. With great reluctance and after considerable probing, the station house officer revealed to the DM that the ten men arrested the night earlier (which had sparked of such a powerful protest) had been released by the courts the same morning. Further questioning revealed that the police had framed charges against them not of murder, arson and rioting, but of the most minor offence of them all—violation of curfew—and the courts had let them off after a fine of fifty rupees each.

The DM cannot recall being more enraged in his life. Everyone was stunned to see the normally restrained officer explode, shouting about the police's deceit and open partisanship and their not being fit to wear uniforms. He warned he would chase them right up to hell if the ten men were not rounded up again within one hour. The police officers rushed back into town, and the ten accused men were rearrested. The DM and SP this time personally supervised the preparation of documents for the courts.

However, it was then the turn of the sessions court to release the accused on bail within a week. The Muslims, who had by then been rounded up in the bomb case, were refused bail for over a year. The DM went to see the district judge, and said, I have never tried to interfere with the judicial process. But here—the same riot, the same offences, the same Sections—how can there be two such openly different standards for people of two communities? It is not an ordinary case, it is the question of the faith of a whole community in the system of justice in our country.

But the district judge refused to even discuss the issue with the DM.

Complaints also came in about excesses in Muslim bastis during the house-to-house searches. The DM visited the houses to find that it was as though a tornado had swept through the homes. Everything in the houses had been smashed, torn or burnt by the search teams—the TV and radio, mattresses, furniture, artifacts, everything. An old woman, around seventy, took off her kameez and salwar to reveal deep lathi marks across her body from the shoulders down to the ankles. The DM ordered strong action against the guilty policeman, and such complaints then did not recur.

After several nights, when peace had returned to the whole town, from one mohalla every night came the same report—stones are being thrown from a nearby mosque. The residents were outraged. Look at how dangerous these people are, they said. Even after all that has happened why don't they let peace return?

Though the mosque was so far from their homes that it was physically impossible for throw stones thrown to reach, the residents stubbornly refused to listen to reason, having been blinded by wanton irrationality. The DM tried to break through this wall by jocularly suggesting that if the people in the mosque could really throw stones the distance of half a kilometre, and that too along winding lanes, their names should be entered for the Olympics. But the people of the mohalla were neither amused nor convinced. Tension mounted again to breaking point.

The suspicion of the SP centred on an elderly resident, a member of a Hindu communalist organization since his youth. But there was no proof. Until one night, when as usual the DM and SP rushed to the mohalla at around 3.00 a.m., they found a broken cup among the stones. Without warning the SP marched into the house of the elderly man and found five other cups in his kitchen to match the broken one. On the second storey of his house, the SP encountered an unbelievable sight. Near his bedroom window was a large trunk full of stones. The old man would stay up every night until everyone else in the neighbourhood had retired, then he would begin to throw stones at the windows of his neighbours. As they would gather angrily outside their homes, he would shout, look at these hateful people. Even after all that has happened, they are still throwing stones at us.

But probably most of all, the DM would remember a young man whose humble thatch hut had been razed to the ground in the riots. Days later, when some normalcy had been restored in the town, the DM sat with him and others among the ruins of their homes and lifetime belongings. The DM assured them with whatever conviction he could muster, do not worry, we will build your house again, and all will be well once more.

Hearing him, the man suddenly broke down, sobbing loudly and inconsolably like a child. The DM felt the sharp sting of tears in his own eyes. Finally, the man said, everytime there is a riot in this town, my hut is burnt down. With great difficulty, I rebuild it, and it is burnt down once more. Tell me, how many times will you rebuild my house?

The DM renewed his pledge to do all that was within his power to help rebuild the lives of the victims of the riot. He called the local leaders of the communal parties and said, I know that it is your aim not only to try to destroy the lives and property of people of the other community at the time of riots. You wish even more to see their wounds fester as they continue to suffer helplessly with their loss. I throw you a challenge. Those whose lives you have taken away, I cannot bring back. But I promise you, those who remain, the district administration will ensure that they are much better off than when you set out to destroy them.

And so, to the young man who had wept so inconsolably, and all other poor residents of the old bustees, who constantly lived in terror of the next flashpoint that would set ablaze their humble belongings, the DM made the offer to move into the new part of the town. Here, new mixed colonies were planned where they could live in security. A large number agreed, and the district administration acquired land, allotted plots and sought out grants and loans for them to build new homes.

Those who had lost an earning member, or their commercial establishments, often no more than a rented ramshackle kiosk in the town's outskirts, were allotted the most commercially valuable sites in the heart of the town, pucca shops were built, and allotted to them on ownership basis.

The next change in government predictably saw the DM shifted out of the district. Some years later, on a new assignment in the state headquarters, he once again toured the town of Khargone. In the evening, he made a quiet, sentimental journey to the new part of the city, to meet the young man who had wept so inconsolably years earlier because his home had been burnt down in every previous riot. He asked him what had happened when Khargone was rocked by riots once again when the Babri masjid was razed in December 1992. The man said quietly, for the first time in my life during a riot, I was safe.

It was not the young owner of the new tenement whose cheeks were wet with tears that evening.

THE THREATENED SETTLEMENT

At the edge of the prosperous coastal town of Tenali, in Guntur district of Andhra Pradesh, is a small humble settlement of a few tenuous mud and thatch houses. These homes have been built on mounds which are surrounded by thick black slush of the city's refuse.

To a casual visitor this settlement seems no different from the slums in which more than a quarter of the town's population live. But, if one actually wades through the slush to reach the homes, it becomes apparent from the manner the residents negotiate their movements, that at least in one way this colony is different from most. Almost all its residents are blind.

The story of how this settlement was conceived and fostered is one that touched us, who stumbled upon this colony, with a sense of wonder.

Suryanarayana was fifteen years old when he lost sight in both his eyes, the result of a reaction to medicines administered to him for an attack of typhoid. Before this, he has memories of a commonplace but happy and carefree childhood, cycling, going to his village school in Kupravoor, rolling old cycle tyres down its dusty paths with a stick in a makeshift game popular with village children. All of this came to a sudden, cruel stop when blindness suddenly shrouded his world in darkness.

Forty-five years later, speaking to us, he recalled how he lost his eyesight. There was no rancour in his voice, as he went out of his way to absolve the doctor who had treated him for typhoid, of any blame for his blindness. He was a good doctor, he repeated to us. It was not his fault that I became blind. Maybe it just had to happen.

Suryanarayana's distraught father, a woodcutter and small farmer, sold a portion of their tiny plot of agricultural land, to raise money for his son's treatment. He took him to a number of doctors in big hospitals in the bewildering metropolises of Bombay and Delhi, but none of them gave Suryanarayana and his father any hope. He would be blind for life.

As he tried to grapple with the prospect of his son's dark future, Suryanarayana's father learnt that there was a blind school in the neighbouring town of Rentachintala, and he admitted his son there. Suryanarayana spent a year in the school, where above all, he reflected on how to rebuild his world. Slowly, the boy came to terms with his great loss.

From the beginning, Suryanarayana was clear that, more than anything else, he did not want to depend on anyone, not even on his father and brothers, to have to feed and take care of him. He found that what he was learning at the blind school would not be enough to make him self-reliant. He loved music, and he thought that if only he could learn to play the harmonium, he would be able to earn his living and not have depend on anyone.

After a year in school, he left because he felt there was no time to waste. He went, instead, in search of a guru to teach him music. Meanwhile, the teenaged Suryanarayana earned a living by selling books on trains. In time, he came to hear of the famed harmonium player and singer, Guru Vidyanagaram. He found out where he lived, and one day, he summoned up enough courage to go to his home in Rajamundry. Falling at the guru's feet, he begged him to accept him as a disciple. Although Suryanarayana had no money to offer him, the ageing musician accepted the young man because of his fervour to learn, and his wife cared for him like a son.

Within six months, Suryanarayana learnt to make music on the harmonium so melodiously that his guru decided to send him to perform in village plays. This would help Suryanarayana to earn some money, as well as to hone his art. And so a whole new world opened up for Suryanarayana, which would remain with him for a lifetime. As village audiences sat rapt around the makeshift stage, the historical and mythological epics— Raja Harishchandra, episodes from the Ramayana, Kurukshetra and so many others—all came alive to the mellifluous strains of the music that Suryanarayana produced. It was indeed a great gift.

In time, Suryanarayana's guru passed away, and not wanting to be a burden on the widow, Suryanarayana left their home. Once again, he earned his living selling books on trains. In between, invitations continued to come in for village concerts and plays. It was these that he looked forward to; they lighted up his life.

In many of the performances of a small rural drama troupe which Suryanarayana joined, a young sighted singer would sit with him and perform. The elders in the troupe took a liking to young Suryanarayana, and suggested that he get married to the singer. Both her parents worked as day-labourers and were impoverished. They did not object to the wedding, mainly because no dowry was to be paid. Shortly after the marriage, the girl's parents migrated to Rangoon, never to return.

She was a good wife to him. She took great care of him and gave him two healthy sons. Suryanarayana continued to tour with his drama troupe wherever it went, but once their family grew, his wife stopped travelling in order to take care of the children. The family settled down, first in Rajamundry, then Tenali. But then she died, during a miscarriage, when she was carrying their third child.

Suryanarayana struggled to bring up his two sons. Some friends in his neighbourhood in Tenali spoke to him of their sister Shantamma. An attack of small-pox when she was only three years old had left her blind in both eyes. She had no memories of a lighted world.

Shantamma's father had died when she was very young. Her mother was very poor, and worked as a coolie, a day-labourer. Her elder brothers also went to work when they were older. She would be locked in, and left alone all day at home. She learned to cook, and do all the housework. Her mother and brothers were kind to her, but being over-protective, they would not let her move out of the house alone. They would not let even her go to school. When she became older, neighbours informed them about the blind school in Renchatinala, and once they actually brought an application form for her admission there. She longed to go to the school, but her mother tore up the form, and would not hear of it. What use could schooling be to a girl, and more so, to one who was blind?

Shantamma had no training in music, but she had a beautiful voice. Partly in order to cope with her loneliness, she taught herself songs that she heard on the radio, or those that blared from loudspeakers. After Shantamma and Suryanarayana were wed, they became a popular duo in drama troupes. They were also invited to sing religious songs in many a village. Shantamma's brothers helped out in all this.

Shantamma had no children of her own, but she brought up Suryanarayana's two boys like her own. They were good sons. When they married, Suryanarayana and Shantamma themselves encouraged the boys and their brides to move away. The ageing blind couple was too proud to be a burden on their sons.

The elder boy took up a job in a textile factory, but this closed down and he now works as a carpenter in Tenali. The younger boy found it much harder to find work. He moved to Guntur, and Suryanarayana and Shantamma saved money to buy him a sewing-machine to set up a tailoring shop. They learnt from someone that even this did not work out, and that instead he now plies a cycle-rickshaw to feed his family. But he has not told his parents this himself, and they do not ask, because they do not want to hurt his pride. They have two grand-daughters, who visit them often, and are the joy of their lives.

Along the way, as their boys were growing, the couple also brought home a blind boy Ekkala Sambayya. Suryanarayana had found him sleeping on the railway platform, lonely and uncared for. Shantamma and he decided to bring him up like their own son, and they took care of him for many years, until he was a young man. Ekkala was born blind. His family did not care for him, and he was left to his own devices, confined to home most of the time. At the age of five, he decided that he could take this neglect and humiliation no longer, and he left home. The little blind boy found his way to his village railway station, and after two days of hunger, boarded a train. He did not know where he alighted. It was at the major railway junction of Tenali. Here he learnt to beg on trains to earn a living. Until he was twelve, the Tenali platform was his home. It was after this that Suryanarayana took him into his family.

But, with the years, as Ekkala grew to adulthood, not wanting to be a burden, he returned to his vocation of begging. The shame of being a beggar, and the passengers' taunts, still wounded him deeply. Often, he thought of suicide.

It was the plight of people like Ekkala which led Suryanarayana and Shantamma to think about setting up a sangam or organization of blind beggars. I was gifted, with education and music—says Suryanarayana—so we never begged for a single day. But the condition of most blind people, and even more so of those who are forced to beg, moved us into thinking that something should be done for those like us, who were less fortunate.

Discrimination was part of every aspect of their lives. It began even with the search for a place to stay. Landlords would refuse to rent out their tenements to them. These blind people would not be able to keep our rooms clean, they would say. It would not be safe to have blind tenants. Many were, therefore, forced to sleep in railway platforms, or under trees. Women and children were never safe. Begging was also a humiliating and insecure means of livelihood. Beggars were constantly harassed by railway officials and policemen. Often, those engaged in begging would leave before dawn, by the first train, and return home late at night, never sure of how much money they would bring home each day. Many days they would have to go hungry.

Though they had been dreaming of starting this organization, it was only 1983 that it finally took shape. Suryanarayana and Shantamma saved money from a concert they had given, and they organized a big lunch for blind beggars. News of it was passed around by word of mouth, and on the appointed day, more than eighty people found their way to Suryanarayana and Shantamma's home. Not all who came were blind. Some were physically disabled. Some were women abandoned by their husbands. All of them begged for a living. All of them were welcomed. These outcastes of society, till then strangers to one another, decided at this occasion, to come together, to help themselves and each other to build a new life. No person, no organization, had come from outside to motivate them to start the sangam. It was their own idea, their own decision. There were many dreams that they shared, which they hoped that their sangam would accomplish, of education for their children, of giving up begging for dignified livelihoods. But for any of this to be possible, a beginning would have to be made with getting their own homes.

The organization was given a name, the Sri Venkateswara Andha Viklangula Seva Sangham, and initially, had thirty-four members. Suryanarayana took advice from the educated people he knew, and they suggested that the organization be registered. The couple set more and more money aside from their concerts, and Suryanarayana's persistence paid off. It took only two months for the society to get registered.

Suryanarayana and Shantamma then motivated the members to give up begging and take to other means of earning money. Over the years, some twenty people have left begging, and instead sell toffee, peppermint, pins and bindis on trains. The sangam has formed its own cultural troupe, and earns money through concerts and village plays.

But the most cherished dream of the group, to have their own homes, has remained paramount. For eleven years, they petitioned successive district collectors, political leaders, municipal authorities, even the chief ministers of Andhra Pradesh, for allotment of land. The officials and politicians would sometimes hear them out, some would make assurances, but for these long years, nothing happened. Suryanarayana and Shantamma, with their thinning band of supporters, refused to give up hope, nor to let their efforts flag.

In the summer of 1994, eleven years after that momentous lunch in Suryanarayana and Shantamma's home, their persistence at last paid off. Mainly as the result of the advocacy and support of the MLA Nadendla Bhaskar Rao, the state government bought twenty-nine acres of the agricultural, temple-endowment land of the Chinaravara temple, on the outskirts of Tenali, and allotted three acres of it to the members of the sangam. The district administration also gave small grants of Rs

1,000 to each of the thirty-two people who were allotted these house-sites. Many took loans of around Rs 10,000 each from local moneylenders at exorbitant rates of interest, but none of this seemed of consequence. What mattered was that they were able to begin work on the plots for their homes, at last.

They hired tractors to level the land, and began construction. For two months, the members of the sangam were elated. They felt that their days of pain and humiliation were a thing of the past.

But then the rains came.

The site where the plots are located is shaped like a bowl, and the surrounding drains rapidly flooded it. This was aggravated by a huge canal skirting the land. Three former extremely powerful lessees, who had rented in the land from the temple trust and cultivated it for years, refused to vacate, and continued to till it by force. They repeatedly flooded the land by opening the canal sluice gates. One of them, Nageshwar Rao, even tried to plough down the sangam members' half-constructed homes with his tractor, but Suryanarayana and other residents stood firmly before it, and at last he turned back.

The former lessees took the case to local courts, lost, and the case moved on to the Hyderabad High Court. But the society of blind beggars did not give up. With the help of a lawyer Subramaniam based in Hyderabad, and savings from innumerable concerts, they doggedly fought the case in the High Court. In 1996, eventually the High Court passed an order in their favour, restoring the land to the state government.

But even five years later, at the time of writing, the order of the court has not been implemented. Using a battery of time-tested instruments—political clout, money and threats of violence—the former lessees remain in illegal possession of the land and continue to cultivate and flood it with impunity. Some twelve of the most steadfast members of the sangam, including Suryanarayana and Shantamma, raised tiny mounds of land amidst the flood and drain waters, and have built their homes on them. These mounds are transformed into islands for several months in the year. Repeated petitions to local officials and municipal authorities have not succeeded in securing the eviction of the former lessees.

Instead, two years ago, the sangam members' problems were further compounded when local authorities decided to divert the large open drain carrying the sewerage and refuse of the city into the patch of land in which the blind beggars' colony is located. As a result, their homes are now surrounded not just with water but waist-deep sullage. After returning from a day's work, when the residents have to cross this to reach their homes, perched on the mounds, they have to first call out. The residents on the other side shout out to them in reply. Being blind they follow the sound of these voices to guide them across. The ground beneath the slush is soft and sticky, and often has pieces of glass, on which they have to step. To move forward on the treacherous path, they also have to part the thick overgrowth of water hyacinth covering the drain waters, and the garbage. Often, they may stumble, and any provisions they may have purchased fall into the sullage.

Over the years, they have petitioned the authorities in the city to at least provide a small bridge or culvert so that they can be saved from walking through the water and the city's drainage. None of them have been responsive. Recently, a young sub-collector told them, since you beg, why are you asking me for the bridge? Why do you not beg for an extra ten rupees every day, and build the bridge yourselves? Although this group has been buffeted, humiliated and ignored for many long years, they are surprisingly without rancour. And, yet, this one thoughtless remark by the young sub-collector has wounded them immeasurably.

It was a group of young social workers, in the course of a poverty survey in Tenali, that encountered the colony of blind beggars. They did not know what to expect, as they waded through the thick slush to reach the tenuous islands that are the beggars' homes. They heard, with initial disbelief and then with wonder, the story of how the group came together and of their long and dogged search for a better life.

A bond grew between them, the ageing blind residents of the threatened settlement, most of whom earned a living through begging, and the youthful social workers.

It was these young people who led me to the home of Suryanarayana and Shantamma, where the entire group of residents gathered together in the fading evening light. At the end of the meeting with us, in which they recalled the story of their struggle, they asked why one of the social workers was missing; we told them that he was hurt in a motorcycle accident. The residents spoke among themselves and decided to offer a special prayer for the boy's early recovery. They all stood up, and said a long, elaborate and fervent prayer for him, with a passion and sincerity that I have rarely encountered.

As they prayed, a stillness fell over the evening. After the prayer ended, and we left their homes, it was dark. One of my young friends gave words to all our unsaid thoughts—that in this humble colony of forgotten people, we received far more than we could ever give.

NOTES

AFTER BHOPAL

I am deeply grateful to Sunil who agreed to share his story with me. I stand indebted to Abdul Jabbar, who introduced me to Sunil, and who has stood by the survivors of the Bhopal nightmare and not allowed their hope for justice to die. I am also very grateful to Sathyu who has taken care of Sunil during his difficult times, and continues to do so, apart from his significant work for the survivors of the tragedy. I thank Sadhana Pathak and other colleagues in Action Aid Bhopal. For details on the industrial and legal aspects of the gas tragedy, I have depended on two recent publications. The first of these is entitled *The Truth of Bhopal* (1999), edited by Kailash Shrivastava 'Admi', and published by Abdul Jabbar, Convenor of the Bhopal Gas Pidit Mahila Sangh. The second is an unpublished backgrounder entitled 'Surviving Bhopal: 15 Years On' (1999) by a Fact Finding Committee whose enquiry is still under way.

HOUNDED LIKE CRIMINALS

I thank the women of Mehboob-ki-Mehandi for sharing with me their experiences. I have changed their names to protect identities. I am indebted to my friend and sensitive reporter, researcher and writer Anantakrishna, who fought the case of these women, and told me their story.

Also to writer and social worker Prema, who introduced me to the women, and assured them that I was worthy of their trust. I hope that I prove myself to be so.

A HOME ON THE STREETS
I am grateful to Anand (name changed at his request) for sharing with me his story. Also to Father George Kollashany and his dedicated team at BOSCO, the brothers and lay staff, for their affection, compassion and respect for the 'little men' of the streets.

SCAVENGER NARAYANAMMA
I owe a debt to Narayanamma for sharing with me her life history, and both her pride and her shame. I am in deep solidarity with Wilson in his struggle, and grateful to Mr S.R. Sankaran and others who have added to its strength. I thank Sandeep, Anjiah and my other colleagues in ActionAid Hyderabad, who have resolved to partner the struggle to end this social evil.

A BATTLE AGAINST FORGETTING BHAGALPUR
For all the facts in the story about the events of the riot, including about the Chanderi pogrom, I have relied completely on the report of the judicial commission of enquiry instituted by the Bihar state government. The report was submitted in 1995.

I am grateful to Malika for sharing her tragic story with me, despite having repeated it hundreds of times over, in her unending search for justice.

I thank my friend, forester Javvad Hassan, who belongs to Bhagalpur, and suggested that I write this story. The story was one that was particularly heartbreaking for me to research, because of the extent of human savagery and official abetment of injustice that it reveals. I could get myself to write about only a fraction of what I learnt of the brutality. I am grateful to my ActionAid colleagues Pushpendra, to Rizwan, and the humane relief workers of Gandhi Peace Foundation, Bhagalpur, for their support. And I thank Dr Farooq Ali, Professor of Zoology, Bhagalpur University, for his profound words that a people who choose to forget their history are bound to repeat it.

A WOUNDED HEALER: LIFE WITH HIV

I am grateful to Deepak Kumar Singh Leimapokpam for sharing his story with so much honesty. He insisted that he did not want to maintain his confidentiality. I thank also his young and brave friends in MNP+ for giving me of their time and thoughts. I am thankful to my colleagues in ActionAid, Guwahati, Prasanna Pincha and Gopen Moses, for introducing me to Deepak and supporting his work in MNP+.

THE LAND OF JAGTU GOND

This story was written as a tribute to the young tribal man whom I encountered during my first tenure as SDM, who had fought this long battle for almost two decades. To protect his identity, I have altered his name and even the location of the story. The events of the legal battle in this story are entirely true, but the personal relationships are partly fictionalized, because this was written originally as the script of a film to be made by Saeed Mirza, but which never saw the light of day.

Many readers have asked me whether Jagtu ultimately

got back his land. In most such cases, throughout tribal India, people like him would not have succeeded in such a struggle. The odds are too strongly weighted against them. But it is almost a miracle that the young tribal man after whom Jagtu is fashioned, did get back his land, several years later. This was the result of a combination of factors, most importantly his very rare persistence and courage. But it was also made possible by the unusual support he got from a young officer years later, who dropped all his work to rush to the village and give him possession of the land on a day on which, by chance, there was no stay order from any court. The court battles continue to date, but the young tribal man now fights them from a position of strength, because he has become master of a vast tract of some of the most valuable land in the district.

THE SECRET WOUNDS OF JATIN

I am grateful to gentle Jatin for telling me his story. The people of Ashagram have become part of my life, their lives a testimony of human courage and dignity, for the way that they rebuilt their lives from the ruins of the most brutal stigma and exclusion. I owe a lifelong debt to Hiralal Sharma and his band of dedicated colleagues who have made the dream of the people of Ashagram their own, and given it their life.

WEATHERING THE STORM IN ERSAMA

I am grateful to Prashant and Vasudeva for sharing with me their stories, to Ambika Nanda for helping me understand the nuances of Oriya. I cherish the wonderful work that my colleagues in ActionAid, Bijay Kumar, Basant Kar, Dharitri Patnaik, and many others have undertaken for the community-based rehabilitation of widows and orphans who have survived the tragedy.

THE HOME BENEATH THE RIVER
I wrote this story when I was divisional commissioner in Bilaspur in 1997. I am grateful to Nanhe for speaking to me of his life.

THE SECOND RAPE
I am thankful to the intrepid fighter for women's rights, Kavita Srivastava, for introducing me to Bhanvari Devi and to Bhanvari for sharing with me the details of her struggle.

DOOMED TO BONDAGE
I am grateful to Bilasini Banchod to have had the patience, grace and forbearance to share with me her painful story, despite her deep despair. I am grateful to Sharanya for assisting me as interpreter from Oriya (even though her own eyes frequently brimmed over as she spoke). I am indebted to my ActionAid colleagues Bijay Kumar, Umi Daniel, Sharanya, Alok, and Kumkum as well as Sandeep Chachra and Anuradha, for their dedicated work with the survivors of drought and chronic hunger in Bolangir and the brick-kilns of Hyderabad, to the young researcher and film-maker Rupashree who is tracking the lives of the survivors and their partners in the NGO Vikalpa, who suggested that I meet Bilasini.

THE SEAL OF THE SARPANCH
I am deeply indebted to the activists of Mazdoor Kisan Shakti Sangathan, whose steadfast commitment to values

of justice and transparency, and simple and austere
lifestyles, have greatly inspired me for long. I regard their
battle for state accountability as one of the most
significant struggles against injustice in independent India.
I am grateful to them for introducing me to Pyarchand,
and to him for sharing with me the details of his story.

1984: STILL SEEKING JUSTICE
I am thankful to Sardarni Harnam Kaur and Daljit Kaur
for sharing with me their experiences of the 1984 riots,
despite the deep anguish these memories aroused, and to
dedicated trade unionist Than Singh Josh for introducing
me to them. In reconstructing the events of those fateful
days, I was aided not only by their descriptions, but also
by the important report of a Joint Inquiry into the Causes
and Impact of the Riots in Delhi from 31 October to 10
December, People's Union for Democratic Rights (and)
People's Union for Civil Liberties, 1984, entitled 'Who
Are The Guilty?'.

PAYING FOR HIS TEA
I am grateful for the dedicated young team of Aashray
Adhikar Abhiyan, under ActionAid Delhi, for their
wonderful work with the homeless people of Delhi, and
for introducing me to Shabir Singh; these include Indu
Prakash, Bidhan, Paramjit, Jeet Kaur, Dhananjay, Shalini,
Jagdish, Jaishree, Cherian, Adil and Aditya. I am thankful
to Shabir for his grace and hospitality, and his readiness to
share his story with us.

THE LAMINATED MARKSHEET
I am deeply grateful to Rajendra for having participated in

the first meetings that we organized of the Bedia community, to reflect on social reforms to free their women, and for his courageous public declaration of his situation. I admire Geeta for her strength to give up the security of her livelihood, and with Rajendra to break the taboos of her community, to rebuild lives of dignity and choice. I am also indebted to Mr S.C. Behar, then Principal Secretary in the Government of Madhya Pradesh, who supported this work with great sensitivity and empathy, and to my former colleague of the Directorate of Scheduled Caste Welfare, Government of Madhya Pradesh, Dr Ghanshyam Gupta, for his learned insights and for factual details about the Bedia community.

THE THREATENED SETTLEMENT
I am grateful to Suryanarayana and Shantamma to have spoken to me of their inspiring lives. I owe a great debt to my young colleagues in ActionAid India, Sandeep, Sunanda, David and Bahadur, and Tom and Rajeshwar of Praxis, for having discovered this colony of blind beggars, for the respect and solidarity that they extended to them, and for their resolve to join their struggle and share their dreams for a better life.

It would all begin with the construction of a small bridge.